BRAIN FU*KED

7-STEP SYSTEM TO STOPPING A NEGATIVE SELF-TALK MINDSET THAT IS HURTING YOUR MIND AND GUIDING POSITIVE THINKING, POSITIVE EMOTIONS, AND POSITIVE DISCIPLINE TO YOUR LIFE

ALEC MOONEE

CONTENTS

Introduction	9
1. What You Need to Know About Negative Self-Talk	19
2. The Demons in Your Mind	46
3. Why Is Negative Self-Talk Not Always Bad	64
4. Introspecting the Right Way	78
5. Step 1—Commit to Taking Action	106
6. Step 2—Change the Narrative	118
7. Step 3—Write a Thought Record	130
8. Step 4—Build Your Self-Worth	138
9. Step 5—Communicate	152
10. Step 6—Practice Mindfulness and Meditation	162
11. Step 7—Take Care of Your Body	182
Conclusion	193
Resources	197

© **Copyright 2020 - All rights reserved.**

The content contained within this book may not be reproduced, duplicated or transmitted without direct written permission from the author or the publisher.

Under no circumstances will any blame or legal responsibility be held against the publisher, or author, for any damages, reparation, or monetary loss due to the information contained within this book, either directly or indirectly.

Legal Notice:

This book is copyright protected. It is only for personal use. You cannot amend, distribute, sell, use, quote or paraphrase any part, or the content within this book, without the consent of the author or publisher.

Disclaimer Notice:

Please note the information contained within this document is for educational and entertainment purposes only. All effort has been executed to present accurate, up to date, reliable, complete information. No warranties of any kind are declared or implied. Readers acknowledge that the author is not engaged in the rendering of legal, financial, medical or professional advice. The content within this book has been derived from various sources. Please consult a licensed professional before attempting any techniques outlined in this book.

By reading this document, the reader agrees that under no circumstances is the author responsible for any losses, direct or indirect, that are incurred as a result of the use of the information contained within this document, including, but not limited to, errors, omissions, or inaccuracies.

The Daily Morning Habit Checklist

(Don't Finish Your Morning Without This)

THIS CHECKLIST INCLUDES:

- 8 Habits you cannot take out of your morning routine.
- 8 Reasons why it will change your mood about your day.
- Implement these habits within the first hour of waking up.

The last thing we want is your day ruined because you didn't have the best start.
To receive your Daily Morning Habit Checklist, Visit this link (PS: It's Free):

https://tinyurl.com/HabitChecklist

"We were free of self-judgment when we were babies, and yet at some point, we developed a sensitivity that taught us to react with self-consciousness and negative self-talk."

— ELAINA MARIE

INTRODUCTION

Right from when we are little kids, we start to learn things that will make up for our adult lives. Not all of these are positive, and some can trigger negativity in one's life. This negativity arises from negative thoughts, which can result in depression, anxiety, worry, and stress.

Negative thoughts can affect your self-esteem, and it can even prevent you from getting to the heights of career or making progress in your relationship and your overall life.

Let us use this story as an example:

Linda had been in a relationship with Mark for five years. However, she had a negative outlook on the relationship, and regardless of what Mark did, she was never satisfied and was never happy. This was because of her negative perspective, which led her to magnify only the negative actions taken by Mark and completely ignore the positive.

With time, the environment in the relationship became fully negative, and her constant focus on negativity led to frustration, anger, and eventually, the end of the relationship.

This is a typical example of how negative thinking can prevent progress in a relationship and untimely death of the relationship. However, it can also affect your career in this same manner—for instance, passing off a promotion because you think you are not good enough and it comes with an increased workload.

The worst part about negative thoughts is that it is subtle, and this makes it difficult for people to tell when it is ruining their lives.

To help you understand better, check out the following statistics:

- The National Science Foundation states that an average individual has around 12,000 to more than 50,000 thoughts daily. And of these, negative thoughts make 80%, while repetitive thoughts make up 95%.

- More than 70% of girls around the ages of 15 t0 17 stay away from typical day-to-day activities, like going to school when they are not happy about their looks.
- Three-fourths of girls who have a low level of self-esteem take part in negative activities like smoking, unhealthy eating, and so on.

However, that is not all. There are still so many consequences to negative thinking, which makes it essential that you deal with it **now**. Some of these consequences include the following:

- It prevents you from progressing.
- It hinders you from achieving your goals.
- It kills your confidence.
- It leads you to live in fear.
- It triggers boredom and predictability.
- It enhances your levels of anxiety.

If you are familiar with any of these, it means you need to do all you can to start eradicating this dangerous habit today.

However, if you are like many people out there, you may not even know you have a problem, and these negative thoughts are subtly wrecking your life. Or perhaps you have tried to get rid of negative thoughts by yourself only to realize that you were unable to make any progress. Well, regardless of what the case is, there is a tried and trusted set of secrets that can help, and we will discuss them in detail in this book. It is known as the *seven-step system*.

The seven-step system is the system you need to stop negative thoughts and get your mind and life in a positive direction. To ensure ease of understanding, I have broken the book into two parts.

The first part will be looking at how you can prepare yourself for the seven-step system, and it will cover a few crucial topics, such as the following:

- What negative thoughts are and how you can spot them
- Causes of negative self-talk
- The consequences of negative thoughts
- Types of cognitive distortions that cause negative thoughts
- Benefits of negative thoughts
- Introspecting the right way

The above topics are what we will be covering in the **first four** chapters. Starting from **chapter five**, we will take a deeper look at the seven-step system, which includes the following:

INTRODUCTION | 13

- Step 1: Commit to taking action.
- Step 2: Change the narrative.
- Step 3: Write a thought record.
- Step 4: Build your self-worth.
- Step 5: Communicate.
- Step 6: Practice mindfulness and meditation.
- Step 7: Take care of your body.

There are many recipes out there that promise to help you eradicate negative self-talk and fail to deliver. This is because many of them fail to realize that negative self-talk is something that you attack from various angles if you are serious about correcting it.

Many of these thoughts are beliefs that have been ingrained into our subconscious over the years, and in order to correct them, you will need to repair yourself physically, emotionally, and mentally. The seven-step system understands this and encompasses strategies that heal you from all of these angles.

I have been where you are, and I have experienced firsthand how destructive negative thoughts can be. My name is Alec Moonee, and I am a motivational speaker who has a passion for teaching others how to live a meaningful and purpose-filled life.

All these began for me a little after my 26th birthday when I was in a car crash. I had some severe injuries, but I was able to pull through. However, this event changed a lot of things, including my perspective. Before my accident, I found it hard to come up with anything of value to stick with, and after the accident, things became worse. I almost made a self-prophecy of doom with my constant negative thoughts.

However, I learned something crucial during my time in the hospital, all thanks to the other patient I shared a room with. Even though he lost the battle, he showed me how positivity and happiness could make a huge difference in life. People were always around him because of the positivity he radiated to the end.

This gave me a new mission, and after my recovery, I did tons of research online and interviews with other experts on meaningful and happier living. Then I took a degree in communication from Southern California University to help improve my public speaking skills, and I have not looked back ever since.

I decided to share what I have learned with others who are experiencing the same thing I have but are unable to find perspective themselves. I spend most of my time organizing webinars and workshops that aim to encourage and motivate people to lead a more meaningful existence.

The seven-step system was one I put together after

many years of research. The great news is that you don't have to go through the near-death experience I went through in order to get it. I have put all you need in this easy seven-step system and how you should go about it.

However, it is not a magic formula that automatically fixes all that is wrong with your life. You will still need to put in the effort, and it requires a ton of commitment and time. However, if you are willing to do the work involved, I am certain that you can get rid of all those negative thoughts and start to live a meaningful life filled with positivity.

Remember that negative thoughts are subtle and extremely dangerous. It is not something that you can leave behind and say you would get rid of tomorrow. The longer you allow your mind to be clouded by this form of thought, the more damage it causes to every aspect of your life.

This means you need to begin practicing the seven-step system today. Don't wait till tomorrow because the more time you waste, the deeper the damage it causes, and the harder it is to free yourself. You deserve a life filled with positivity, happiness, and meaningfulness. Don't let the negativity tell you otherwise.

Are you still interested? Then do read on.

"Attitude is a choice. Happiness is a choice. Optimism is a choice. Kindness is a choice. Giving is a choice. Respect is a choice. Whatever choice you make makes you. Choose wisely."

— ROY T. BENNETT

1

WHAT YOU NEED TO KNOW ABOUT NEGATIVE SELF-TALK

Negative thinking has to do with one thinking in a manner that offers no benefit. There are cases where these kinds of thoughts may affect your life negatively. This is because negative thinking can contribute to unhealthy conditions like anxiety, depression, and stress.

Every one of us engages in negative thinking. The only difference is the frequency at which we have these thoughts. However, when you continuously have these negative thoughts, it can affect your overall life.

For instance, constant negative thoughts can destroy the confidence you have in yourself. This happens when you keep on seeing the negative sides of things to the extent that it prevents you from taking action. It can also wreck your mental health and leave you battling with anxiety and depression.

WHAT CAN WE CATEGORIZE AS NEGATIVE THINKING?

Negative thinking has to do with thinking non-beneficial thoughts. However, due to the nature of these thoughts, it is easy to confuse the normal worry that everyone experiences for negative thoughts.

When you are feeling down about the loss of a loved one or about issues in your relationship, it does not count as negative thoughts. It is normal for everyone to deal with thoughts like these at some point in time. However, when these thoughts become constant and repetitive until they begin to affect one's ability to perform daily tasks, then it is a problem.

To put it into better perspective, negative thinking is a form of thinking that does not help you achieve something you desire. In most cases, it may even prevent you from achieving it.

For instance, let us presume that you want to go ask your crush out since you desire love and happiness. The negative thought "I'm boring this won't workout" will not work to your benefit. It will also make it more difficult for you to make a move and get into a relationship in the first place.

So why does this happen? Here are a few reasons:

- When you think "I'm boring this won't workout" and you start to genuinely believe it, your self-confidence dwindles. You also lose trust in yourself entirely.
- Next, it bites into your motivation. When this happens, you are less inclined to take the steps you need to achieve happiness and love. In this case, it means you don't even ask your crush out or go into any relationship in the first place. This is because you already have the belief that it is something you can't achieve.
- Ultimately, you don't go after the happiness and love you desire. All of these are a result of your negative thoughts.

Negative thinking fails to elevate your mood and can even worsen it.

If we go on with the scenario covered above and you feel like you are boring plus you have made a negative conclusion of something that hasn't even happened yet, then the negative thought "I'm boring this won't workout" will make you feel worse.

Here are a few reasons why this happens:

- When you believe that you are boring and have made the conclusion that the relationship won't work it starts to make you feel weaker, undesirable, and helpless. This already makes you feel worse.
- Next, it wrecks your self-confidence and the trust you have in your abilities. Since you believe your situation can't be salvaged, it starts to make you feel helpless and bite into your self-worth. This happens because you feel you are powerless against your predicament.
- Just by genuinely accepting the negative thought "I'm boring" you can feel worse in numerous ways. It can contribute to feelings of unhappiness, sadness, and depression.

It is of no use and does not improve your life. It can even make it worse.

Still continuing from our scenario above, the instant you fully accept the negative thought "I'm boring this won't workout," it makes it more difficult for you to find what you are looking for. This is particularly the case since it is already worsening your mood in various ways.

It is crucial to note that the negative thought is not useful to you since it does not pose any benefit and will only worsen your mood. When you determine how these thoughts are not beneficial to you in any manner and even sometimes worsen things, it's best to completely eradicate these thoughts.

Now that you understand what negative thoughts are and what we can categorize as negative thoughts, let us investigate what causes these thoughts.

WHAT CAUSES NEGATIVE SELF-TALK?

There are three common reasons why people engage in negative self-talk. They include the following:

Fear of the Future

Most people are scared of the unknown. This is a normal fear for humans as we fear the future and things that may come along with it. Will the future bring joy, or would it bring disaster?

The typical individual has a deep-rooted worry about the future and invests time into thinking about what the future holds for them. A lot of people get past this by staying positive and believing that things will fall in place if they keep pushing. However, other people worry and are overtaken by fear of disaster, failure, and embarrassment.

We invest too much of our energy worrying about those things that have not occurred and most likely never will. This is like paying for a loan we have not collected yet. This fear can be a constant source of negative thoughts in the life of anyone.

Worry of the Present

In addition to being scared about the future, we worry about the present too. We worry about the security of our investments or those things that are precious to us.

We worry about things going as they should during our absence. Something as simple as worrying about whether you left your keys behind at home or whether you forgot to turn off the tap in your bathtub can lead to constant negative thoughts. Worry stems from the fear that we are forgetting something vital.

Sometimes, we fill our minds with irrelevant information, making it difficult to recollect those things that are crucial. This overload of irrelevant information, alongside the constant fear of forgetting, can trigger a never-ending cycle of negative thoughts. This is particularly the case if this happens in excess.

Shame in the Past

Many of us have done things that we are not proud of. This could be something embarrassing or extremely shameful. Sometimes, we do things hoping that they go one way, but they go in the opposite direction. These mistakes can result in shame occasionally. When this happens, it is easy to get trapped in feelings of shame, thereby triggering incessant negative thoughts.

However, in addition to these, there are a few habits that can trigger negative self-talk. We will be looking into some of them below.

HABITS THAT CAUSE NEGATIVE SELF-TALK

Thoughts that don't give value to us are known as negative thoughts. We receive negative messages from external sources, and sometimes they influence how we should feel and act. Many of us learn these negative self-messages right from when we were young and continue to develop them as we grow old.

Soon, they become a part of our subconscious and happen automatically. Since these thoughts can be challenging to deal with when they have attached themselves to your subconscious, your best bet is to keep them afar.

An excellent way to do this is to point out any habits you may have developed that may encourage or aid negative self-talk. Pointing out these habits and curbing them may help eradicate physical and mental issues that may arise in the future.

Below are a few habits that could be encouraging negative self-talk that you were not aware of:

Failing to Deal with Issues in Your Relationship

If there are severe issues in your relationship, the best thing you can do for your mental health is to deal with these issues. If you fail to do so, it may lead to constant negative self-talk.

Let us take the life of Lizzy as an example.

Lizzy was dealing with problems in her relationship with John. For a while, they had not been on speaking terms, and just last night, she found out that he was seeing another woman even though he rejected her sexual advances a few hours earlier.

Before she found out he was cheating, she was already feeling inadequate and sad. She couldn't concentrate anymore and was always blaming herself for all that was happening in this relationship. Now, with the new information, she began to feel way worse and began to believe she was no more attractive.

This further strengthened her feeling of inadequacy and negative self-talk she experienced.

This scenario is the case for many people with issues in their relationships. When there are issues, the first thing they do is to hold back to avoid more issues. They do this with the hope that the problem will fix itself so long as they don't try to talk about it.

However, when there are issues in your relationship, you need to sort it out for the sake of your mental health and relationship. If you fail to do this, you may deal with serious negative self-talk. This is because by leaving problems unresolved, you start to develop a negative environment around your relationship. This environment is what triggers negative thoughts and further worsens the issues in your relationship.

Poor Health Habits

If you have poor health habits, it will eventually affect your health. Now, when your health is not in great shape, it is impossible to feel good about yourself, which can trigger negative self-thoughts.

For instance, if you are dealing with a severe health issue, it is normal to be concerned about the future. You may start to think of how your life will end soon, which can trigger negativity.

Your health can affect every aspect of your life. And if you fail to give yourself the appropriate care, it starts to affect your mental health, which then triggers negative self-talk that you are forced to believe. The best way to prevent this is to find a healthy regimen to ensure you stay in great shape always.

Being Isolated for Too Long

When you spend too much time by yourself, it can cause you to think negative thoughts. When we spend time around other people, we can easily distract ourselves by interacting with them.

However, when we spend time alone, we are left to interact with ourselves, and from here, the negative self-talk may arise. When we interact with other people, we are urged to restrict our self-talk because our brain needs to pay attention to the person we are interacting with. Merely learning to spend time with more people around you can help tone down these negative thoughts.

Not Requesting Assistance

One of the best ways to deal with negative self-talk is to request for help. If you have the habit of not seeking assistance when you require, your negative self-talk may worsen.

Asking for help can be a huge step and might seem like a lot. After all, it is not easy letting someone else see you as weak. However, merely requesting assistance from an expert or friend can be all you need to disrupt the cycle of negative thoughts. This is because of the validation that comes from someone agreeing with what you are experiencing.

If this does not seem easy for you, a better way would be to do it in little steps. For instance, you could call a friend anytime the negative thoughts comes and instead of saying hey I need help, more like hey what do you think of this? You don't need to go all-in before you begin to enjoy the positive benefits that come with requesting for help.

Failing to Engage in Self-Care

In addition to physical health, it is essential that you don't ignore your wellness. This is where self-care comes in. Simply put, self-care is the care of one's self. It has to do with all actions taken deliberately to care for our emotional, mental, and physical health.

This is something that a lot of people ignore, but the fact is that if you are in peak physical condition and ignore your mental and emotional health, it could still result in damaging negative self-talk.

When you engage in self-care, you automatically tell yourself that you are important and worth the effort. Whenever you can, take a step to let yourself know that you are significant. With time, you will start to feel the positivity come in.

Failing to Accept That You Deal With Negative Self-Talk

As we covered earlier, every one of us experiences negative self-talk. However, the first step is admitting that you have them. If you fail to do so, you will refuse to see that these thoughts are problematic and refuse to do anything about correcting them. With time, the situation will worsen, and you will find yourself stuck in a vicious cycle of negative thoughts.

Refusing to accept the adverse interactions that run through your mind and pretending to be fine can result in you feeling worse than you are.

Hanging Around Negative Individuals

Regardless of whether you like it or not, you tend to become more like the individuals you spend the most time with. This also applies when it comes to negative thoughts. If you hang around negative people, you are eventually going to become negative too.

Negative people create a negative environment around them, and if you spend too much time with them, you will soon start to see negativity as a normal phase of life. This means if you are battling with negative self-talk, one of the best steps you can take is to point out these kinds of negative people and stay away from them.

If you want to get more positivity in your life, a good habit to adapt would be to surround yourself with positive individuals. This way, you will learn to be kinder and gentler to yourself.

Dealing with negative thoughts does not have to be a complicated process. You can simply point out and work on the habits we have listed above if you are serious about stopping all the negative self-talk.

CONSEQUENCES OF NEGATIVE THINKING

When you allow your negative self-talk to roam freely without doing anything about it, things can become bad fast. Eventually, you will start to deal with consequences. This is where your brain starts to rewire and get Brain Fu*ked.

Negative thoughts can affect the overall quality of your life. They can affect how you act and how you behave. Knowing this, let us look at some of these consequences below:

It Stops You from Achieving Your Objectives

Negative thoughts can make it harder to achieve the objectives that you have set for yourself. In worse situations, it can make it completely impossible. If you have objectives, negative thoughts can demotivate you and push you away from these goals.

Take, for instance, the following scenario:

Paul was offered a new job with the company he always desired. This job had been his dream for so long, and now things seemed to be falling in place. However, the only downside was that he had to relocate from the USA to Germany.

Soon, he began to have the usual negative self-talk and say the following: "What if the job is not all that?" "What if I lose the job?" "How do I leave the country and begin afresh?"

The more he thought about it, the more he started to see the difficulties in his plan. Soon, he let go of the idea entirely and stayed back.

Like Paul, many suffer this consequence of not achieving their goals if they deal with constant negative thoughts. They can make objectives harder to achieve and can stop you from achieving them.

It Breaks Down Your Confidence

Uncontrolled negative self-talk can impede your capacity to see things from the right perspective. In turn, it starts to trigger a reduced level of self-confidence in you. One of the core reasons why negative self-talk creates a haven for low self-confidence is that it triggers other issues.

Some of the types of negative self-talk that may damage your self-confidence include the following.

- "I am so stupid"
- "I am not smart."
- "I am such a loser."

These are examples of negative thoughts that, when constantly repeated, tend to gradually break down your self-confidence. It exhausts you and leaves you unable to take action when you desire.

It Leads to Shame

Constant negative self-talk can trigger feelings of shame. With time, these feelings of shame become overwhelming and start to affect your everyday life.

Some of the negative self-talk statements that can cause this include the following:

- "I am not a good person."
- "I don't deserve happiness."
- "I am useless."

The above are a few kinds of negative self-thoughts that can bring about shame. This is particularly the case when done consistently for a long period of time. When you include "I" in this form of negative self-statements, it strengthens your belief of shame and goes beyond just feeling shame alone. It opens you up to other downsides along with shame.

For one, it leaves you susceptible to perfectionism. When your negative self-thoughts are based on shame, you will always strive to be perfect in all you do so that you don't get to experience this feeling of shame. However, because perfectionism is impossible for anybody to achieve, it only results in more frustration. What's more, shame-based negative self-talk prevents you from accepting your mistakes, which makes your entire situation worse.

Then because you strive to be perfect, you also grow to expect the same perfectionism from others around you. And when they are unable to meet this level of perfectionism, which is what will happen, you begin to judge them. Soon, they start to see you as arrogant, proud, and difficult to deal with, thereby making it hard to maintain your relationships.

What's more, because you want people to be perfect, you become controlling. You begin to have a notion of how you believe others should behave in order to be as perfect as you want and try to enforce it. However, this leads to you always criticizing those around you every time they are unable to meet your expectations.

Finally, you begin to view these shame-based negative self-statements as a means to protect yourself from shame. But these thoughts are the ones that cause you shame and make it worse, thereby leaving you in a never-ending pool of negative self-talk.

It Leads to Issues in Your Relationship

Negative self-talk can trigger problems in your relationships. This could be in your relationship with your friends, family members, and intimate partners. So how does this happen? Let us look at some of these ways:

1. You are unable to create a connection with others.

Constant negative self-talk will prevent you from being vulnerable to other individuals. This results in you having relationships without any genuine connection. Instead of getting companionship and closure from your relationships, you feel lonelier.

Asides from the issues you may have in creating in-depth connections, your negative thoughts may result in the quicker end of your relationships. If you continue to have negative self-talk about your relationship and partner, it starts to reflect in your relationship.

Now, with this form of negativity in your relationship, you start to blow up the flaws of your partner. This is the case regardless of whether they are true or something you imagined.

For example, let us assume that you and your significant other have a misunderstanding and you pretend like all is fine on the outside. However, inside, you continue to have those negative self-statements pertaining to yourself and your partner with anger and frustration.

With time, this might start to be evident in your behavior, and you lash out about completely unrelated things. Every time you breed this sort of negative self-statement, it could lead to disasters in your relationship.

2. You focus on the negatives.

If your thoughts are constantly consumed with negative self-talk, you soon grow to focus on only the negatives. This is the case even in your relationship. With time, you start to ignore the positive aspects and focus on the negatives in your relationship subconsciously.

For example, Mark had developed negativity about his relationship with his girlfriend. Due to this, his subconscious paid attention to the negative aspects of her even when she did something worth praising.

When you are occupied with negative self-talk, it is easy to ignore the great aspects of things and pay attention to the negatives. There have also been studies carried out to support this fact, and one of these includes a study from John Gottman and his team at Washington University during their study centered on negative thinking.

In this study, they carried out an observation of couples who had negative thoughts about their relationships and those with positive ones. To do this, the researchers used video recorders, which were set up in the homes of the couples.

All each partner had to do was simple. They were to fill a questionnaire provided whenever they observed that their partner did something good. When the researchers collected the questionnaires and compared with the tapes, they realized the following:

The couples who saw their relationship in a positive light observed the same number of positive acts as the researchers. However, those who had a negative self-talk pattern missed half of the positive moments with their partners.

In essence, negativity has a way of eroding one's ability to see the positive side of things.

You Hardly Make Any Progress

Negative self-talk can hinder you from making progress in many areas of your life. It is like how it prevents you from achieving objectives, but it goes beyond that. For instance, it can prevent you from making any progress in your career, even with all the necessary qualifications and skills.

Let us look into some of these instances:

You stumble upon an ad for your dream job that you are well suited for. However, you start to question your capabilities and start thinking about how getting the job is a pipe dream. Ultimately, you don't apply, and another opportunity passes you by.

There is an opening for promotion at work, and everyone is asked to indicate their interest. You are qualified, but you begin to think of all the areas you are lacking. Soon, you change your mind about trying and instead recommend someone else for the position.

Let us cover these points in more detail.

1. You don't take new opportunities. Negative self-talk can prevent you from taking on new opportunities when they present themselves. This could be in the form of not sending that job application, failing to take that promotion, or not going into that new relationship. Negative self-talk can make you lose faith in your skills and prevent you from taking steps to help you move forward.

This is because it makes you believe that you don't deserve any of these new opportunities. Even if you are skilled and the evidence shows that you are good at what you do, you instead focus on your own negative perspective of things, even if it is not true. This form of negativity can prevent you from taking opportunities that will help you get the life you desire.

2. Shelving your job search. The job market is one with a lot of competition, especially in today's economy. However, when you incorporate negative self-talk into the mix, the process can become even more difficult. And because of this difficulty, it may be extremely hard to find your dream job.

Instead of going all out to find the job of your dream, you instead see the reasons why you should not and ultimately shelve the entire idea. Negative self-talk makes you believe your best bet is remaining stagnant as opposed to making any effort and failing.

3. You strive to be perfect in the things you do. As we covered earlier, perfection stems from your negative self-talk. One thing that perfection does is to prevent you from making any headway. Since nobody can truly be perfect, you go all out to be and get frustrated along the line.

This is applicable in your career and even your overall life. Now, when you fail every time you try to be perfect, it reinforces your doubts in yourself, and with time, you start to feel it is better to remain in the same position without any progress.

4. *You lose motivation.* Like we stated before, negative self-talk can result in you losing confidence in yourself and your skills. When this happens, you start to lose motivation in everything you do. This could range from your career, relationship, and overall life.

Ultimately, this could lead to issues in all the affected areas. When you have no motivation to do anything, it is hard to maintain focus and excel the way you should.

It Leads to Depression

Constant negative self-talk can leave you feeling fear, stress, sadness, and frustration. Now, when this happens to your body repetitively, it can start to affect it. When this happens, your body protects itself by employing its defense system to ensure there is no damage to your body. This defense system is known as depression.

Depression is the way your body protects itself from

the dangerous impact of constant negative self-talk and thoughts. Depression can suppress the feelings stated above, but it also suppresses the good feelings, such as love, happiness, and joy.

This is what makes depression dangerous for any person, especially when in a state of depression for a long time. However, it is your body's first step in order to survive. Negative self-talk can leave your body believing it needs to be in a state of depression in order to survive.

You Feel Exhausted and Sick

Continuous negative self-talk is one core reason why many individuals end up with illnesses. There is a huge chance that you can end up sick as a result of negative self-talk. This usually happens when you do it so much until it affects your body and leads to illness.

You Silence Yourself

Constant negative self-talk can result in you hiding your ideas and leaving them unheard. This happens even if you have amazing ideas because you keep talking yourself down. Eventually, you refuse to air out these ideas because you don't want to feel embarrassed or you feel your ideas are not good enough.

You Live in Fear

Fear is an extremely powerful emotion. It keeps you stuck, paralyzed, and unable to take the steps you need. This can result in a constant feeling of hopelessness, frustration, and sadness, which can leave you in danger of feeling depressed. If you give negative self-talk control of your life without any control, it can be an unhealthy landmark for the way you live your life.

It Triggers Boredom and Predictability

You are always afraid, so you like to stick to safe measures. This means you don't go out of your comfort zone, and to a reasonable extent, you know what your negative self-talk will let you do and won't.

For this reason, your life becomes easy to predict and boring. You won't take any risky steps, and neither would you try out new things. You lack any excitement, which is important for a fun-filled life.

It Enhances Levels of Anxiety

Negative self-talk can make you see things that you normally should not, even if they are not real. These things you see can bring about problems that were non-existent in your life before. Soon, you start to feel helpless and unable to deal with everything.

In turn, this can trigger continuously rising levels of stress in your life. And when you are always stressed, you start to feel higher levels of anxiety, which can affect your whole life.

You Feel Regret

When you observe your life later down the road, you start to feel disappointed about all the actions you failed to take. There may be a rising feeling of regret as you look back, wishing you had taken action when it mattered.

It may not seem like it right now, but if you allow negative thoughts to control you, it is going to bring about regrets. You regret all those times you did not take that job opportunity and those days you allowed an idea you have to die. This is what negative self-talk does to you.

WRAP UP

If you have felt any of these consequences then I urge you to keep reading because I am writing this for YOU, to help YOU. You can ignore your negative self-talk or deal with them in a proper way. Leaving them unattended can stall your life and affect your self-confidence and belief in yourself. They can rob you of your potential and leave you stuck in a never-ending hold of despair. Nonetheless, the choice lies within you, and you have the power to decide whether you want that to be your life or not.

"When you change your thoughts, remember to also change your world."

— NORMAN VINCENT PEALE

2

THE DEMONS IN YOUR MIND

Cognitive distortions are the demons of your mind, they are unreasonable beliefs and thoughts that we subconsciously support with time. And as you know, the way you think tends to affect how you feel.

Distortions can bring about negativity in our lives and make us have negative self-talk. And in most cases, they are often almost automatic. This makes it hard to spot them in our everyday thoughts, even though they are causing severe damage to our lives.

The fact that they are not obvious makes them dangerous because it is impossible to make changes to what you don't even know is affecting you. There are many forms of cognitive distortions—this is what we will be looking into in this chapter. However, they all have the following traits:

- They are inaccurate and untrue.
- They can cause psychological damage.
- They are patterns of believing or thinking.

It may not be easy to admit that you may be experiencing distorted thinking. And even though many people don't deal with this form of thinking in their daily lives, the reality is that almost everyone has these forms of distortions at least to a reasonable extent.

This means that so long as you are alive, you may have dealt with a decent level of cognitive distortions at one point or another. This is understandable, and it only becomes a problem when you deal with them on a more long-term basis. In fact, the major difference between individuals experiencing distortions in their everyday lives and those who experience it normally is the capacity to point out and alter these unhealthy thought patterns.

However, like other skills in life, you can improve your capacity to identify these distortions and respond to them properly. This means in order to free yourself from these distortions, the first step is to identify them.

Knowing this, let us look into some of the most

common kinds of cognitive distortions there are. This way, you can determine which relates to you best and take proper steps to correct them.

TYPES OF COGNITIVE DISTORTIONS

Filtering

When you engage in mental filtering, you blow up the negative aspects of an event while you phase or filter out the positive aspects. When this happens, you can pick up only the negative part of a situation even though there are other positive things that occurred. Then, you start to have a perception of reality based on this negativity while ignoring the positive.

For instance, John's boss called him into the office and told him about the last proposal he sent in and how it was a success. He said the client loved it because it was elaborate, accurate, and properly explained. However, his boss stated that there were a few punctuation errors that he needed to be on the lookout for subsequently.

John ignored all of the positive feedback and instead focused on the negative feedback of errors he got. This is how the distortion of filtering works.

Jumping to Conclusions

This distortion is just as the name implies. If you are

one who engages in this, you automatically know what someone else is feeling and thinking. You know why they behave the way they do without them telling you.

You also assume the way someone feels toward another individual, even if they don't say anything. This is similar to one believing they have the power to read the minds of other people.

For example, Mark met Peter for the first time at a networking event and tried to approach him. Peter, who was deeply occupied with his thoughts (since he just got a call that his mother was just admitted), responded hastily as he rushed off to the hospital. Mark took this as a sign that Peter hated him, and he held on to that notion without trying to find out if he was correct. He had already established that fact and stood by it.

Jumping to Conclusions (Fortune-Telling)

This is another form of jumping into a conclusion. Here, you assume that things will turn out terribly based on inconclusive evidence, and you genuinely believe this assumption.

For instance, perhaps you feel a little pain in your stomach, and you just assume that this is the sign of a kidney problem and you will feel worse by morning. But the truth is, you have not even gone for any test, and you can't say for certain that it is more than stomach pain.

There are instances when this kind of distortion can transform into a self-fulfilling prophecy. Say you wake up late to work one morning and you keep telling yourself you are going to have a bad day. Then, you don't even try to make up for the lost time, and for that reason, you get to work extremely later than you should have. At work, you get screamed at by your boss and slammed with a query. This most likely happened because you kept forecasting how your day was going to go, and the universe listened.

Fallacy of Fairness

This distortion lets you assume you have a clear understanding of what is fair or not while others don't agree with what you believe. The inability of others to see things from your perspective leads to feelings of resentment in you.

Another way to define this is a rigid outlook on what you believe is fair in life. When you fall into this cognitive distortion, any behavior that doesn't conform to your beliefs will cause anger and anxiety. It is an obsession that you must overcome.

In some cases, the fallacy of fairness in an individual is a result of their upbringing. When you see something happen while growing up, you expect it to remain the same even when it doesn't have to.

For example, if you have parents and neighbors who always see a movie every Saturday, you might start expecting the same from your partner. If your partner fails to do this, you begin to see them as unloving and uncaring.

When you exhibit signs of the fallacy of fairness, you will find yourself making conditional assumptions. Some examples of these conditional assumptions include the following:

- "If they value me, they will get me a better office."
- "If he loves me, he will come to take me out."

The definition of how things should happen often prevents you from seeing the bigger picture in life. You remain rooted in your perspective of how life should be, forgetting that things won't always go your way because life isn't fair.

Blaming

Blaming is one of the most natural forms of cognitive distortion you can engage in. Many individuals don't want to take responsibility for their actions, so they must always have someone to accuse. When you feel frightened, hurt, or in pain emotionally, there must be someone who has caused these feelings.

This is a form of blaming in which you make yourself out as the victim. This may be a result of a lack of proper training during childhood. If you're not taught the importance of taking responsibility for your actions, you will make others do so.

This may stem from a life of luxury in which you have someone taking care of your needs—like a maid. As you grow, you expect others to know what you need as an individual and give the right responses to these needs.

In other instances, blaming may also involve seeing yourself as being responsible for the pain others experience. When you notice any form of unhappiness in anyone, you're quick to blame yourself. It doesn't matter if it is something beyond your control.

Blaming yourself for everything that happens can result from your childhood. If you were the oldest sibling, then your drive to protect your younger siblings can result in this cognitive distortion. It can also be a result of bad experiences during childhood.

Experiencing deaths in the family, fights, or accidents can make you take responsibility for preventing anything terrible from happening. As you grow into an adult, you grow with these beliefs. You fail to realize that not everything is your responsibility and keep blaming yourself when things go wrong.

Global Labelling

Global labeling is a situation in which you have a one-dimensional view of the world. When engaging in global labeling, you pick one or two traits, qualities, or characteristics in making a conclusive judgment. It is common for individuals to use global labeling on themselves, others, or a group.

For example, if you fail a test, you consider yourself a failure. You overlook all the other tests you passed and use this single failed test to define who you are.

The same applies when dealing with others. If a friend forgets to get you something from the store, you label them as inconsiderate, regardless of all the good things they did earlier.

The global labeling of groups is something you may be very familiar with. This is because many people engage in this form of cognitive distortion. It often involves labeling people based on their gender, sexual orientation, race, and so on.

In most cases where you engage in the global labeling of groups, it often leads to disrespect of such groups.

You focus on how you view these groups and forget about humanity. Global labeling usually makes things sound worse than they are.

Fallacy of Change

This is a cognitive distortion in which individuals assume that their happiness or circumstances depend on the possibility of another individual making a change. It implies that the actions of others control some essential aspects of your life. In most cases, this cognitive distortion is noticeable in relationships.

In promoting the fallacy of change, individuals will often pressure individuals to get the desired change. Due to this cognitive distortion, many people face a lot of disappointments. As you focus on getting others to change, you turn a blind eye on yourself and lose control of your life.

The fallacy of change in most cases occurs when an individual is trying to change a situation or an intimate relationship. A fallacy of change in situations happens when you avoid taking action with the hopes that "things would change." Some of these thoughts in this cognitive distortion include the following:

- "If Mom were around, he wouldn't talk to me in that manner."

- "If I had a car, I wouldn't be late for lectures."

These are some simple examples in which you avoid making any effort at creating the change you desire. In changing intimate relationships, it can occur in both personal and romantic relationships. You still feel hurt when these needs are not met without explaining your needs to your friends or partner.

To promote the change in an intimate relationship, people often use strategies such as the following:

- Withholding
- Demanding
- Blaming

Emotional Reasoning

This is a cognitive distortion in which you believe that your feelings are truths you must accept. For example, if you feel that you are a failure, then you are a failure. This cognitive distortion suppresses rational thinking in individuals, regardless of the lack of validity.

A significant reason for this cognitive distortion is due to falsehoods in our beliefs and emotions. When your emotions reflect these falsehoods, then it creates the emotional reasoning cognitive distortion. Understanding that your emotions can be misleading is crucial in identifying this cognitive distortion.

Consider a situation in which you accidentally bump into someone while walking down the road. If you hear someone calling out to you, you may feel yourself getting angry. The thought that comes to your mind might be "I apologized, so why is he/she still calling out to me?"

What if you dropped your wallet after the bump? Or what if you look familiar to the individual? These are the reasons why your emotions are often inappropriate.

Emotional reasoning is often a result of our need to get our brains to function faster. When the brain works faster, you get to achieve more, but you also run the risk of making mistakes. When you react to situations in an instant, you are likely to fall into the emotional reasoning.

Control Fallacies

The control fallacy results from an imbalance in the sense of control you feel you have over your life. At the extremes, an individual can either assume they are in complete control of everyone around them or being hopeless without any form of control. The first extreme is a fallacy of internal control, while the second extreme is a fallacy of external control.

The fallacy of internal or omnipotent control occurs when you assume you bear the burden of everyone around you. It is the belief that everyone around you depends on you for their happiness. Therefore, any form of neglect or mistake on your part may induce feelings of fear, rejection, or loneliness in others.

If you fall into this category, you feel responsible for meeting everyone's needs and making every wrongdoing right. When you fail to do these things, you experience a strong sense of guilt.

The fallacy of external control is one that causes you to remain in one spot, unable to make any meaningful progress in life. It is a cognitive distortion that creates a belief that you're powerless in shaping how you want your life to be. You take the stance that your pain, failure, or suffering is someone else's responsibility.

Due to the fallacy of control, many individuals often develop other forms of cognitive distortions. These include blaming, mind-reading, catastrophizing, polarized thinking, personalization, and filtering.

Heaven's Reward Fallacy

This is a cognitive distortion in which a person believes that there is a reward for every action. These actions are usually in the form of self-denial or sacrifices an individual makes. The distortion feeds on the belief that there is a force in the world responsible for taking note of your deeds and rewarding you accordingly.

Many people who exhibit this cognitive distortion usually judge the world as being fair. That said, we live in an unfair world. A world in which the hardest worker may not always get the best rewards.

Heaven's reward fallacy usually results in high levels of disappointment and frustration due to the unfairness in the world we live in. This is because most of these individuals never get any form of reward—except on rare occasions through luck.

Always Being Right

An individual who believes that their opinion is absolute is a perfect example of this cognitive distortion. They don't consider the opinions or feelings of other individuals when they engage in discussions or debates. They are willing to go to any extent to prove that whatever opinion they have to offer is correct.

To such individuals, your feelings are of no importance. They prioritize being right, and they tend to overlook the hurt and pain they cause others in the process. This cognitive distortion usually has a negative impact on the ability to maintain positive relationships with others.

Catastrophizing

When you engage in this form of distortion, you always expect disaster to happen regardless of the situation. It is also known as magnifying and can also manifest as the opposite called minimizing.

When you magnify, you use what-if questions anytime you hear about an issue and imagine the worst-case scenario. For instance, what if my car crashes? What if I get a terminal illness?

For example, you write a proposal for a business idea and only realize, while you are delivering the proposal, that you missed out a few points. Nonetheless, the proposal goes great, and you get the deal. Your business partners are ecstatic and tell you how well you performed. However, all you can think about are the few points you forgot to include in the proposal.

You have succeeded in magnifying a little mistake and blown up a little issue into a gigantic one. All these cognitive distortions are unhealthy for anyone. Continuously grooming these habits can lead to anxiety, stress, and even depression. So how does this happen? Let us find out in the next section.

NEGATIVE THOUGHTS AND DEPRESSION

As we stated earlier, depression is the body's defense system, and constant negative thoughts is a fast way to get your body into depression. Chronic negative thinking can lead to stress, which can cause damage to the mind and body, which forces it to go into a state of depression.

When your body goes into this state, it turns off all of your body's emotional responses. Depression tones down the effect of negative thoughts on your body by ensuring you don't feel fear. However, it turns off all other useful emotions like joy, love, and happiness. At this point, it becomes a problem.

In summary, if you want to free yourself from depression, you need to deal with the negative thoughts that cause fear and trigger your body's need to go into depression. By stopping negative thinking habits, you can turn off depression.

It is best to note that symptoms of depression can be in the form of irritability and anger. If you are always dealing with these symptoms, you may be dealing with depression.

NEGATIVE THOUGHTS AND STRESS

Stress is triggered by a range of factors like finance, problems with a loved one, difficult job, among many others. It could also be a result of accidents, loss of a loved one, and illnesses.

However, there is also something subtle that can trigger stress, and this is negative thoughts. It can be difficult to identify these triggers because many people are not even aware that their beliefs, feelings, and thoughts can elevate their levels of stress.

This kind of stress is dangerous and can bring about problems like heart disease, anxiety, depression, and high blood pressure. To deal with this kind of stress, your best bet is to eradicate negative thoughts.

"It is only when we take chances, when our lives improve. The initial and the most difficult risk that we need to take is to become honest."

— WALTER ANDERSON

WHY IS NEGATIVE SELF-TALK NOT ALWAYS BAD

To anyone seeking help in overcoming negativity, these negative thoughts automatically become a bad thing. On the other hand, every form of positive thinking is something they wish to adopt. One thing many people fail to do is to stop and ask, "Is this the right assumption?"

When you take the time to answer this question, certain things become more apparent to you. Two things stand out: (1) positivity without limits is a bad thing and (2) negativity can sometimes be helpful.

When you put it in the form of constructive self-criticism, you can reap the positive benefits of negativity. In such instances, it causes you to question your actions and take responsibility for them. This includes accepting your bad decisions as a fault on your part.

For many individuals, they use positive thinking as a form of protection against taking responsibility. This is what usually leads to acts of blame-shifting. It is a way to avoid the feeling of shame and despair that they may experience when they realize their wrongdoings.

Rather than face these feelings, they avoid confronting it and look for an easy way out. If you want to avoid these situations, then you must learn to strike a balance between your positive and negative thoughts. Another thing you must do is to determine the proper application of constructive thinking.

LIVING IN MODERATION—COMPLEMENTING POSITIVE WITH NEGATIVE THINKING

In helping you understand that not all negative self-talk is terrible, it is important also to let you know that there is a need for moderation in positive thinking. While negative thinking can let you see some of your flaws, an overreliance on positive thinking can also be a way to conceal these flaws.

In trying to achieve specific goals, positive thinking can make you blind to all possible outcomes. Instead, you focus only on the result you have in mind. If you're trying to make a sale, positive thinking can make you convince yourself that you will close the sale.

Although this is an outcome everyone wants, is there a 100 percent assurance that this will be the outcome? This is where the negative self-talk becomes crucial. It is a way to help you seal all the loopholes that can prevent you from achieving your goals.

Through positive thinking, most individuals become complacent. This means they overlook the issues that may come up in trying to achieve their goals. The focus on a future with the results you desire prevents you from being proactive in taking the right steps and decisions to secure these results.

Another significant problem of positive thinking is that it often focuses on perfection and not progress. This is why it can sometimes be ineffective and lead to frustration in other situations. When you fail to achieve the exact results you desire, you fail to notice how far you have gotten.

A more effective approach in life is a combination of positive thinking with negative thinking. A perfect balance between these two types of thoughts creates a form of "realism" in your approach toward life. How does this work?

- Start by engaging in positive thinking. This is essential in helping your mind wander toward the things you want to come true. These are your innermost desires.
- Second, you engage in a controlled form of negative thinking. This is crucial in determining the obstacles that can prevent your goals from becoming a reality. Through this combination, you're able to create attainable goals and also make plans that you can use in achieving these goals.

When you perform this process using an unreasonable goal, you're able to identify the flaws in them. This makes it possible to change these goals early on before they lead to frustration in the end.

When learning to live life by maintaining a balance between your good and bad thoughts, there are some actions you can take. One thing you must note is that in dealing with these thoughts, being on any extreme is not a good thing. Regardless, it is easy for anyone to fall on the negative extreme of the spectrum.

To give a better understanding of this, the information in the previous section is crucial. This is why you need to develop certain habits to help you live a healthy life.

This is one in which you can maintain a positive outlook and eliminate the negative bias you may have.

This is a form of training you give your brain, and it takes a bit of time to master this process. Some of the steps you can take include the following:

1. *Remain Conscious of Your Thoughts*

As you journey toward striking a balance, there will be periods when you notice yourself giving room for your negative bias. These are periods when your mind is on autopilot and you need to take back control. To ensure you're always in control, you must learn to be mindful.

Through mindfulness, you can remain conscious of the various events happening in your mind. To maintain your focus in the moment, you need to practice mindfulness. This is a form of training that keeps you aware and conscious of your thoughts.

As a result of your mindfulness training, you can start making conscious efforts to promote positive thoughts in your mind. This is especially useful in situations when you start noticing negative thoughts creeping in.

2. *Do Things That Make You Happy*

Time is a limited resource that you must manage effectively. When you have a full-time job or work multiple jobs in shifts, it can be challenging to create time for yourself. This is because you also need to create time for your family.

Therefore, the first step you must take is to learn how to manage time. If you don't have a schedule, create one now. Using a schedule, you can learn to eliminate activities that don't have any positive impact on your life.

With the additional time that you create for each day, focus on doing something you're passionate about. Spending time doing things you love will help boost your positivity for the day. In most cases, you should perform these activities early in the day so that they set the tone for the rest of the day.

If you're having difficulties creating time in your schedule, then you can consider waking up earlier than usual. You can also choose to reduce your overtime by an hour to make room for your passion.

3. *Learn to Look for Positives in Life*

A common reason why many people have negative thoughts is that they fail to appreciate the good things in life. If you fall into this category, then you need to start spending more time looking for the positive aspects of life.

What do you take the time to notice each day? Are you continually feeding your mind with the negativity you see on the news? A simple action, such as taking a walk in the park, can give you a positive outlook for the day.

There are other positive things you can notice—a friend welcoming a child, a graduation ceremony, a wedding, and so on. What is something good that you can focus your mind on today? This is a question you must ask yourself.

4. *Live Healthily*

It is common knowledge that money can't buy health. Also, there is no way you can maintain a positive outlook in life when you're struggling with health challenges. This is why you need to do what you can to maintain good health.

The best way to do this is to practice healthy habits. Such habits include the following:

- Exercising regularly
- Getting adequate sleep
- Eating a balanced meal

These are some of the essential habits you must develop for a healthy life. Creating time for exercises and getting adequate sleep isn't an option; it is a priority. Once you start maintaining a healthy lifestyle, you begin to notice the benefits, both physically and mentally.

With a healthier body and mind, there is little room for stress and worries. By eliminating these, you can minimize the negative thoughts flowing through your mind.

5. *Spread Positivity*

If you want to maintain positive thoughts, then you can start by having a positive influence on those around you. There are numerous ways to do this, so you just have to pick an option that works. One way is through little acts of kindness—offering to help a neighbor walk the dog, complimenting a coworker, helping a stranger, and so on. Regardless of what you choose to do, spreading positivity will have a significant impact on your mindset.

CONSTRUCTIVE SELF-CRITICISM FOR DEVELOPMENT

One area through which negative self-talk can help is through constructive self-criticism.

In aiding development, constructive criticism offers a means of learning. One reason this is achievable is that constructive criticism is specific. When you engage in it, you focus on a particular part of your life or action that you need to change.

This is what differentiates it from criticism through negative self-talk. When criticism stems from negative self-talk, it is usually vague. The vagueness of the negative criticism is one of the reasons why it has lasting unwanted effects on an individual.

Another benefit of constructive criticism is that it gives you a clear picture of what you need to work on. Since it focuses on a specific part of your life, you have a path or direction you can follow in addressing the issue. In the case of negative criticism, its vagueness makes it difficult to point at what you need to change.

For many individuals, since there is no way to change how they feel, they can only struggle through the adverse effects of the criticism. Finally, the specific nature of constructive criticism also makes it an excellent means to achieve your goals.

When criticism from yourself or another individual points out a specific flaw, you can determine if it relates to you or not. As you engage in constructive criticism, here are some things you must always remember:

- It allows you to identify, learn from, and correct your mistakes.

- You become more productive as you look for new ways to improve your actions.
- You're more thoughtful since you learn to empathize and see things from the perspective of others.
- You learn to be honest when talking to yourself.

When engaging in constructive self-criticism, there are two options. These options are as follows:

- To protect yourself and cause ruin
- To take responsibility and promote improvement

The first option is a situation in which you try to downplay the importance of an event or shift the blame for a failure to others. Although you feel good about yourself afterward, you also create room to make the same mistake.

In the second option, you take full responsibility for the failure. Doing this will cause you to work toward growing as a person and to stop making excuses for your actions. If you do decide to take a step toward making constructive self-criticism, the following are actions you can take:

1. *Focus on Things You Can Change*

An excellent constructive criticism is one that focuses on things that you can change. In most cases, focusing on changeable behavior is the right move. For example, if you have trouble waking up early, then you can learn to sleep early.

To make this possible, you can stop watching television toward bedtime so that there is no distraction to keep you awake for too long.

2. Create the Right Environment

Certain failures and mistakes are often a result of environmental factors or circumstances that can be avoided. If you fail to deliver a project before the deadline due to issues with your computer, then changing the computer can prevent problems in the future.

The critical step here is to ensure that you don't make the same excuse on multiple occasions. Look for a way to prevent the excuse so that it doesn't hinder your actions in the future.

3. Learn Self-Compassion

Constructive criticism can be a difficult burden for some individuals. This is when self-compassion becomes crucial. Self-compassion offers an opportunity for you to enjoy the positive effects of constructive self-criticism without beating yourself up as a failure.

FINAL THOUGHTS

This chapter may seem **presumptuous** and **disparaging** to most readers, but it is important to look at things from **multiple perspectives**. As a self-help author that you've turned to for help in overcoming negative thinking, this chapter contains facts that you **must** know.

When you only focus on the positive-thinking movement, it is usually difficult to notice yourself sliding into the unwanted area of victim-blaming. This is something everyone must avoid.

It is okay to feel bad about certain things. The fact that you're maintaining a positive mindset doesn't imply that you need to express guilt over these honest feelings. You must understand that everyone is different.

Therefore, the needs of an individual will differ from those of another. The attitudes you consider as being right may be wrong to another person. Nevertheless, you're not to blame for your decision.

This is one thing you must remember when trying to create a balance between your thoughts. A subtle yet problematic effect of being extremely positive is the possibility of wallowing in guilt over your actions. By choosing to tread on the room between your good and bad thoughts, you can maintain a more beneficial approach.

In the wording of these thoughts, my goal is to encourage you to remain critical. Be critical of the things you read, hear, and see. Your background will differ from that of another individual, and as a writer, I can't boast or presume to understand your unique background.

As you keep this in mind, there may be some tools in this book that won't give you the results you desire. Regardless, all the ideas in this book are worth exploring. This is because, from each idea, you can reposition yourself on the correct path to attaining wellbeing.

"You are the sum total of everything you've ever seen, heard, eaten, smelled, been told, forgot - it's all there. Everything influences each of us, and because of that I try to make sure that my experiences are positive."

— MAYA ANGELOU

4

INTROSPECTING THE RIGHT WAY

One of the most important aspects of getting rid of your negative self-talk is having an in-depth knowledge of yourself that is what introspecting is. What would you say if I asked you to write or talk about yourself? Will you be able to do that clearly and convincingly?

Self-awareness is a much-talked-about topic, and it is effortless to assume that you have a handle on it. I mean, if you didn't know yourself, who else does? You need to understand that there can be different degrees of self-awareness, so it is more useful to focus on becoming more self-aware.

A less-talked-about topic is the different ways to gain more understanding of yourself. Indeed, the best resource you can turn to when you're trying to become more self-aware is yourself. However, getting other people's feedback can be instructive.

What you do with the feedback you get from people around you—colleagues, friends, and family—could make all the difference. When you go through the process of self-examination by introspection and reflection, you can gain more self-control if you do it the right way. Otherwise, the result would be the opposite.

In this chapter, you'll learn what self-awareness means and what you must become more aware of. You'll learn possible ways you can become more self-aware. We'll be focusing a lot on how you introspect and the right way to do it.

To begin, the next section is about the ways through which you have developed your personality, what influenced them, and what helped to form your behaviors. This is important in understanding what changes you have gone through and how to keep track of their effect on yourself.

MAKING OF THE SELF: PERSONALITY DEVELOPMENT

All that we are and all that we can define ourselves by are the results of three things. First, there is the human being as a biological animal. The basic building blocks of personality and distinction are passed down to you genetically.

Alongside genetic inheritance, your personality encounters another formative factor. Your environment, especially how you relate with it, shapes genetically contributed features. Who you live with, who you play with, who you speak to, how you're treated, and what the society values and condemns—all these come to bear on the person you become.

Man's evolution further refines and solidifies his identity and perception of himself. Now, evolution is not just the Darwinian transformation of man into a higher species of animal. Your diversification caused by contact with and response to a functional or dysfunctional environment is a major factor in personality formation.

How you react to your environment, how you deal with influences, and how you respond to stimuli in the society all contribute to who you are. Knowing what you make of these experiences becomes the ultimate proof of self-awareness.

I'll give you an example. I could get work done fast, and I get a lot of amazing feedback because of this. My supervisors loved my speed of delivery of assigned tasks. My bosses couldn't help using me as a model for the other staff. These did not matter as much as how I responded to it.

My response to all these pats in the back was overconfidence. Then came the change in my attitude, which I only noticed when I quit my office job for a remote position years later. I would put off finishing a project until the last minute. I was working from home, so there was a lot else to keep myself busy with. Eventually, I started handing in work later than the deadline and requesting extensions. This is just a simple illustration of how what we perceive and how we respond to it ultimately shapes who we become.

WHY WE ACT THE WAY WE DO

A person's reactions, behavior, or fundamental personality is not based on a logical principle or strategy. Professor Antonio Damasio, the David Dornsife Chair in neuroscience and University of Southern California's psychology, philosophy, and neurology professor, has connected insight to our intimacy with what we know, perceive, or experience over time and have come to recognize.

The summary of Professor Damasio's research is that decision-making (and by extension, behavior, personality, and actions) is emotion-based. Professor Damasio has proved that a person does not act based on logically constructed strategies or principles but merely as a response to stimuli. The nature of this response is based upon collated experience data.

That is proof that the nature of your actions, thoughts, thought processes, behaviors, and overall personality are as a result of what you experience externally and how you interpret it internally.

Of all three factors highlighted in this section, environmental factors are the most pronounced influence on personality. However, the third factor, which is individual interpretation and response to external stimuli, is a more important influence.

The biggest study into the psychological theory of sexuality by Andrea Ganna and his team was conducted by collecting and analyzing DNA from over 470,000 people. Andrea Ganna proved that human sexuality is based largely on a lot more non-genetic factors than the five recognized genes responsible for deviations. Benjamin Neale, a co-author, confirms by saying that both biology and a person's environment can be responsible for their sexuality.

Neale refers to the environment as a range of experiences in a person's development as well as social and cultural factors that could all affect one's behavior.

What You Should Know

A lack of response to environmental change-causing agents and the inability to adjust to social experiences result in the broad spectrum of psychological abnormalities studied under abnormal psychology. Deviations from expected diversification due to experience could arise from the inability of an internal mechanism to function properly.

In other words, if you're not changing (growing, developing, and adapting), then something is wrong or you're not doing something right. No matter how little, all experiences—conscious, unconscious, and subconscious—contribute to the totality of our personality. What contributes even equally is what we do with those experiences. Taking stock of what we have felt, heard, seen, or perceived and relating it with how it has affected us leads to self-awareness.

WHO YOU ARE: SELF-AWARENESS

Physically, if a child suddenly stops to grow or develop, we know at once that something is not right. In the same way, we recognize abnormalities when a person stops or is unable to grow, develop, adapt, and diversify. The whole personal development process, if intentional, is based on what you know of yourself.

What you know will inform you of what to change or improve to develop. Self-awareness helps you implement self-improvement strategies. This is the crux of the whole matter.

Self-development requires self-awareness. Self-awareness is impossible without the two that make it up: self-consciousness and self-examination. Achieving self-awareness is the first step in taking charge of your life and intentionally charting the course of your future by creating what you want. Knowing who you are is the only way to create change in your personality and your thought process, and it gets rid of negative self-talk.

Simply put, to be self-aware is to know oneself. Do you know yourself? Most people think that they've got a handle on this one. You'll be surprised to learn that not a lot of people know themselves as well as they think they do.

What You Should Be Aware Of

To have complete knowledge of yourself, you ought to become more aware of your personality, your behavior, your strengths and weaknesses, your beliefs or values, and your motivation.

1. Your personality: I want to say here that there are not four or five or three clearly defined personalities like most people believe or would want you to believe. There are countless. A person's personality is like a jar of jelly beans with multiple colors of very tiny all-flavored beans that make up the contents of the bottle.

Another way to look at it is by using a color scale or wheel. Between red and blue, there are numerous colors made up of different degrees/quantities of red and blue. Gaining more understanding of your personality makeup is an important aspect of self-awareness.

2. Your behavior: The only thing worse than not knowing your personality is perhaps surprising yourself. Not having full knowledge of your behavior is like going to sleep in your bed and waking up in some other place—you have no idea how you got there.

Be aware of your behavior—how you're going to act in this situation, how you ease off or handle stress, or how you act around friends and family. It involves knowing what would cause you to respond or act in a certain way.

3. Your strengths and weaknesses: You see in movies the first time a superhero (or villain) discovers their super-strength by breaking a door handle or a glass just by holding it. That could happen to anyone who lacks self-awareness.

Some signs that you have poor self-awareness are not knowing how much work you can get done in what time, how much emotional stress you can endure before you break down, or just how strong or resilient you are.

In like manner, not understanding your limitations—everyone has got to have some—is a sign that you lack self-awareness. A self-aware person knows when to give up, what tasks to politely decline, and what places, people, or things to stay away from.

4. Your beliefs or values: This is usually the highest cause of uncertainties at work, in your career, and in life. When you're not sure of what you believe in, you are unable to take a stand or make a decision. Knowing clearly defined values and belief systems is an aspect of self-awareness that you cannot overlook.

5. Your motivation: What inspires you to act this way? What's your reason for taking this job? Why have you suddenly decided to start a blog or read a book on religion? Knowing your motivations is the final piece of your self-awareness. Knowing your motivations helps you focus on your passion, shut out distractions and pressure, and eliminate clutter from your mind.

Benefits of Self-Awareness

Self-awareness is how you become an authority on yourself. Becoming aware of who you are, what motivates you, how you respond to certain things sets your life, passions, dreams, goals, and objectives in perspective. It enables you to focus on what's most important to you. It allows you to value yourself more since no one knows you more than you know yourself. This essentially weeds out negative self-talk.

Self-awareness is an important aspect of emotional intelligence. You obviously cannot lead others when you don't know or have control of yourself. A supervisor who does not understand their strengths and has not mastered their behavior will try to micromanage everyone, boss around their staff, and ultimately achieve very little as a leader. A self-aware teacher can build a result-yielding relationship with their students. They easily understand their students, and their responses achieve a maximum result.

This also helps you become a better customer service

manager or sales executive. All of the attributes of a successful modern leader—interpersonal relationship skills, teamwork, empathy, emotional intelligence, persuasion, and influence—all begin with self-awareness. It is not knowing the job that makes you awesome at it; it is knowing yourself.

I've mentioned that self-awareness helps you define your passions. It also enables you to gain mastery or control of yourself and your actions and not just to live life on a whim. You'll be able to easily transform your thought process and the way you feel when you have total knowledge of yourself.

How to Become More Self-Aware

There are several self-awareness activities you can practice in a timely manner—daily, weekly, or quarterly. These activities do not all work in the same way for everyone. So as you go through them, take notes of aspects, components, or alternatives to them that may work best for you.

I'll give my top five easy self-awareness activities to help you gain a deeper knowledge of yourself.

1. Self-evaluate.

Self-assessment is perhaps the most important way of getting to know yourself. Now, self-assessment works on the principle that no one knows you more than you know yourself. Assess yourself in these three ways: by retrospection, introspection, and reflection. You can do this daily or weekly, but do it as often as possible.

2. Keep track of your action.

Well, even high school students do this one. I find that I can always track my actions, progress, or monitor my response to certain situations by writing a journal. Find time to write in your journal the results of your self-evaluations so that you can keep track of yourself.

3. Get feedback.

Don't be afraid to ask for feedback. This is a wonderful way to know who you are by finding out from people what you did well, what you could have done better, and what they thought about you. Ask coworkers, friends, and family for their opinions. Ask your clients for constructive criticism of your work. Request for written feedback if you feel they might be reluctant to talk with you freely. Be insistent on getting an honest report of not just the good but also the bad.

4. Use self-analysis tools.

Perform psychometric and typology tests to evaluate your personality with respect to other people's. Other tools to use include emotional quotient analyzers and tests and mobile journal applications that you can write on the go if you feel you don't have the time to write on a physical one.

5. *Analyze yourself against existing models and requirements.*

This is not a way to compare yourself with others. It is merely a way to find out how you defer and why and what that means for you. You know yourself better when you know the difference between you and some other model so you can clearly define your values and strengths.

In all this, two things become more significant. First, you must decide that you want to find out the truth. Second, you want to get feedback from people and yourself. This is what is known as self-evaluation.

Self-Evaluation

Self-evaluation is one of the two components of self-awareness. It is known as self-examination, self-assessment, self-analysis, and it also translates to self-reflection. Self-evaluation is the observation, analysis, and documentation of the different aspects of the self: your personality, behavior, strengths, weaknesses, beliefs or values, and motivation.

You'll notice three aspects of self-evaluation: (1) observation, (2) analysis, and (3) documentation. If you do not pay attention to the things you do, how you respond to people, and how they respond to you, the things you're drawn to, then the analysis would be impossible. Be observant. Be awake. Be conscious and intentional. Then when all is done in the day or at the end of the week, take some time to analyze those observations. Make use of a journal to record and keep track of yourself and your progress.

Self-evaluation is not the same thing as self-consciousness. To be self-conscious means to be aware of your environment, your influence on it, and its influence on you. Self-consciousness and self-evaluation come together to give you complete knowledge of yourself.

There are three components of self-evaluation—three ways through which you can assess yourself. The first, *retrospection*, is simple. It involves looking back at past experiences, analyzing your responses to them, and finding out its influence on yourself. The second and third are *introspection* and *reflection*.

This chapter will focus more specifically on introspection and reflection. Given the importance of introspection in finding out who you truly are and what defines you, you must learn how to do it the right way so that you can benefit from it.

INTROSPECTION AND REFLECTION: WHAT IS THE DIFFERENCE?

Introspection and reflection are nearly similar to methods of analyzing the self. A lot of people use them interchangeably. They both have to do with in-depth self-analysis that leads to self-awareness and self-improvement.

What Reflection Is

Reflection is, in some ways, the counterpart of retrospection. It is an analysis of current events to figure out what you did best, what you could have done better, and what are your responses to this feedback and what to implement. In the end, reflection gives you a lesson on the day-to-day approach toward mastering yourself and creating your desired future.

I want you to look at reflection as looking at yourself in a mirror after a day at work. What do you see? How do you look? Do you like how you look? What are you going to do about it?

Reflection implies criticism of yourself. You can start the reflection process by gathering feedback from other people. It doesn't have to be an analysis of your observations. Reflection can be an analysis of other people's honest opinions, sort of like asking someone, "How do I look?" instead of looking in the mirror.

What Introspection Is

Now, introspection is the self-evaluation that you have to do by yourself. It does not involve people's feedback, but it can call up results of reflection done on feedback from others. What introspection means is an evaluation of one's general behaviors, attributes, values, and standards. When you inspect your definitive thoughts, thought process, and feelings and you evaluate the cognition that the mind has of its actions and states of being, then you are introspecting.

When I introspect, I am not merely looking into myself to observe, but I'm also trying to analyze what I discover.

Coming after introspection, reflection will appear as a comparison of your general personality and values to your behavior in the current or a specific moment. Introspection and reflection go together to enable self-awareness, plan your future, predict growth, relate with others, and overcome self-disruptive tendencies.

Periodic introspection is important. Reflection can even be done at every moment. For instance, before you speak or take action, you reflect. You weigh your action or words against your defining qualities and see how they measure up or how they may affect yourself and how it differs from who you are. In a way, self-evaluation happens always, and it helps you take control of yourself.

CHALLENGES TO INTROSPECTING—WHY IS IT SO HARD?

Introspection is easier said than done. In a society like ours, with our need to always be on the go and multi-task while at it, it's easier to live life on a whim than it is to examine ourselves. This is why you find it easier to slide into negative self-talk when something happens than it is to take a break, settle down, breathe, and reflect upon what happened.

Being too busy to take some time and work on your self-awareness is as dangerous to you as disregarding preventive and predictive maintenance schedule for a machine. The result is a spontaneous and unexpected breakdown. This itself will lead to corrective measures, which are more harmful when you hardly even know yourself.

Distractions and interruptions are also challenges. You can agree that sources of distraction in modern society are endless. There is less room for contemplation and introspection now than there ever was before. We have texts to reply to, emails to check, friends to hang out with, families to visit, dates to get ready for, and events to attend. And we have all these on top of the extensive time we spend working.

Even when the time does present itself for self-reflection, we become anxious to sustain a strain of contemplative thought. You simply wouldn't know where or how to begin. It makes excessive working, speed-dating, blundering through life, and general business so much easier when you don't have to sit down with yourself and analyze your feelings or discover your desire for the future. You just don't know yourself, and you have no idea how to begin to know.

What you need is effective time management combined with setting your goals and priorities straight to eliminate most of the challenges to introspecting the right way.

TOP 5 STEPS TO PRODUCTIVE INTROSPECTION

I know there aren't enough hours in a day. I also know that you have a very busy work life that you can barely balance with an even more demanding personal life. I understand the challenges. If your identity crisis has begun to crash into the aspects of your life that you don't want it to, it makes it even more difficult to self-reflect productively.

However, I've made a list of my top five steps for productive introspection. As usual, it is not the ultimate master list; nobody has that. They're more like best practices, but they don't work for everybody in the same way. When you go through it, take notes, adapt, modify them, or use better alternatives that may work best for you.

Step 1: Seek the truth

I've mentioned this in the section on how to become more self-aware. This is a general principle when dealing with yourself. Avoid self-deception, seek the truth, and ask for honest criticism. It is the only way to move forward—the truth shall make you free when you know it. It is the first step to introspecting productively.

Step 2: Make the time

Overcoming the most obvious challenge to self-reflection—too busy, can't make it—is the second step to a productive self-reflection. Do what I do. Balance your work calendar with your personal calendar. Make time in your schedule for having lunch with friends, spending time with the family, and introspecting. Follow your schedule strictly. The more you get to know yourself, the easier you find allocating time for different tasks.

Step 3: Plan against interruption

I could say avoid interruption, but sometimes, it finds you no matter where you go. So I say "plan against." Where are you most likely to run into a friend who'd want to chat? When are you usually alone? What time of the day is your mind surrounding calm? Answering these questions helps you distraction-proof your venue and time for self-reflection. Remember to keep phones and gadgets that may distract your attention at a safe distance.

Step 4: Meditate

Practice meditation that helps to center and collect your thoughts, focusing your mind on specific details you're trying to assess. It doesn't have to be complex. Sometimes, sitting calmly in a quiet place with controlled lighting and some breathing exercises is all you need.

Step 5: Keep track

As I've said before, self-reflection is a purposeful project. Keep track of your progress, resolutions, observations, and the results of your reflections. A journal is best for this. Try to make an entry each day to focus on your self-awareness goals. You can make use of a mobile journal application on your smartphone if it's easier.

Even when introspecting in this way, a lot can still go wrong. Following the steps above will help you start to achieve your self-reflection goals. It is easy to assume that a person who introspects will begin to gain self-mastery and complete self-knowledge. Study shows that not everyone who introspects has positive results to show for it.

This is because there is a healthy right way to do it and an unhealthy wrong way.

HEALTHY AND UNHEALTHY INTROSPECTION

Teaching you to introspect is just as important as teaching you the right way to do it. Productive introspection has the potential to get rid of negativity. It relieves stress, depression, and anxiety and helps you gain control of your life. This is a healthy introspection.

Unhealthy introspection does not give you an insight into yourself. You can spend countless hours introspecting and still not gain self-awareness. What's more dreadful is that the more you introspect, the more depressed, confused, anxious, and less self-knowledge you have. This is when introspection is done in the wrong way. Introspecting the wrong way can confuse how you perceive yourself and bring a lot more negative results than you bargained for.

Unhealthy introspection is a result of a latent cognitive bias, which causes one to agree with reasons that only confirm their long-held beliefs. It's an inability to keep looking for deeper answers when we've found the most obvious two or three.

ASK "WHAT?" NOT "WHY?"

Generally, focusing your reflections on the *why* rather than the *what* is a recipe for unhealthy introspection.

For instance, if a coworker had surprised you with a gift you didn't expect, the right way to reflect on this would be to ask what this means to you, how it makes you feel, and what you can do about it.

Asking *why* questions are not as beneficial as asking *what* because it could mislead your mind into spiraling into directions that do not lead you to more self-awareness and satisfaction. Introspecting the wrong way has a way of making you focus more on your problems and try to lay blames instead of helping you grow healthily.

Healthy introspection keeps your mind open to finding out new information about yourself. The wrong introspection puts you in a victim mentality and keeps you circling around in the past.

I find this best practice of self-reflecting the right way useful, and I hope you do too.

1. When reflecting the right way, it starts with an acceptance and a desire to move forward. So you accept that you're depressed or that you're anxious. Then you try to move on from there by finding answers to questions like "What is happening?" "What am I feeling?" "What am I saying inside my head?" "What other ways can I look at this situation?" and "What can I do to respond better?" Even if it is your periodically scheduled introspecting sessions or in-the-moment reflections of current experiences, ask *what* and *how* questions and avoid the *whys* like the plague.

2. Do not overthink it. Don't go too far. Don't be biased either. When you over-analyze, you're most likely ruminating and no longer introspecting. Overthinking it creates more depression and anxiety, less control over your life, and gives you no peace and satisfaction.

3. Don't focus on depressing things. It could lead to more depression and, eventually, shut down. Don't start the vicious cycle. Over-analysis of the things that are depressing in your life paralyzes you and makes it impossible to take action, respond, or grow.

Identifying and putting a name to your feelings in the process of introspection shows a healthy self-reflection. Being able to transform your emotions into language—and always remember to write them down—as opposed to simply just feeling them, helps us to stay in control.

BENEFITS OF INTROSPECTION

Aside from the obvious benefit of creating self-awareness, introspection can give you an insight on how to solve problems relating to you or other people. If all the gods, all the heavens, and all the hell are within you, then you just have to search within you to find the solution you need.

Introspection also aids self-consciousness. It gives an objective picture of your immediate surroundings—how it affects you and how you respond to it. It also analyzes your expectation of your world. This helps you decide and plan for your desired future.

Introspection takes away the veil that covers most things when we observe from a distance. Close observation and delicate but objective reflection of things open us up to see them as they are. This makes you wiser as in the biblical saying, "When I was a child, I behaved and reasoned like a child. When I became a man, I put childish things behind me." Introspection is a way to learn to grow and become wiser while avoiding mistakes.

Self-assessment through introspection enables you to overcome fears and anxieties. You can create mental peace and positivity by reflecting on what makes you anxious and what you can do about it. That is, how you can best respond to it.

There's a noticeable improvement in emotional intelligence, empathy, and interpersonal relationship skills in a person who introspects the right way. A person who truly understands their feelings and what their desire is can more easily understand how to manage, lead, and relate with people. Introspection opens you up to countless possibilities.

Becoming aware of yourself by introspecting the right way puts you on the right track to shutting up your inner negative self-talk.

PRE-SYSTEM ACTIVITY

Before we start diving into the 7 step system, I have a story. A baby elephant tied to a stake in the ground. When it's a baby there is no way it can pull it out, it is physically not strong enough. So eventually the baby elephant decides to stop trying to tug and run because it knows its efforts are futile. The elephant then grows and become strong and powerful but it remains tied to the thin breakable stake in the ground because that's what it learned as a baby. The Elephant knows its power but won't pull the stake, due to its own self-talk.

Let's take a moment and name the critic in your mind something really ugly and give it crazy lame features. Every single time it says something negative, roll your eyes, tell it to shut up and say something positive. I personally do this and it has changed my life and opened my mind. I urge you before moving forward give it a try. With that being said let's move into what you have been waiting for, The 7 Step System.

"I've always believed that you can think positive just as well as you can think negative."

— JAMES BALDWIN

STEP 1—COMMIT TO TAKING ACTION

Commitment is a quality that you need to dedicate yourself to any activity you engage in. When working on anything in life, including your well-being, commitment is essential for your success. People who exhibit commitment in their actions are those who get results.

You don't give excuses, and you don't accept them either. When you lose your motivation to act, commitment is what gets you through to the end. If you want to learn to stop giving up halfway through an activity, then this is a place to start.

In the face of negative behaviors and self-talk, you can use your commitment as a force to get you through. As you try to overcome your negativity, there will be moments when you experience relapses. It is in these moments that you need to put in everything you have left.

People who commit to learning try harder when they come in the face of obstacles. The reason for this is that they understand that getting past a hurdle is more soothing than giving up in the face of one.

The feeling of accomplishment you get through commitment is also crucial in dealing with negativity. This sense of accomplishment helps you develop self-love, which is a vital part of overcoming negativity.

QUALITIES OF COMMITTED PEOPLE

They Show Passion

When you show passion for anything you do, you will always want to see things through till the end. This is one of the qualities that all committed individuals exhibit. Being passionate will naturally promote acts of dedication and commitment to an individual.

They Are Critical

Everyone can perform a task, but not everyone can complete these tasks to the best standards. For people with commitment, they don't go for superficial results when approaching a job. They focus on getting the best. This approach towards their tasks makes them critical.

They Adapt With Ease

When trying to accomplish a task, the result is what matters. This focus on the result makes it easy for a committed individual to adapt to changes around them. They don't give in to any form of obstacle they encounter but learn to use them to their advantage.

Another way to describe this is as being in harmony with the surroundings. You understand every change that occurs, and you make the most out of it.

They Are Tolerant

Some goals take a long time and require a lot of effort. For many individuals, sticking around to complete these goals isn't an option. This is not the case with committed individuals.

Being tolerant also goes along with patience. These are two qualities that committed individuals depend on to do what they have to.

Commitment is a quality that you must develop as an individual. Once you develop this quality, you are ready for the next step—building healthy habits.

BUILDING HEALTHY HABITS

Habits matter a lot when trying to overcome negativity. The actions you perform every day can have a significant impact on your behavior and thought patterns. Three parts are essential to building a healthy habit, and they include the following:

- Cues
- Routine
- Reward

Cues are the feelings or things that function as the trigger for your habits. For instance, the close of work for the day can be one of your cues for boredom. Your cues are vital in creating or changing your habits, and you must learn to recognize them. When you learn your cues, you simplify the process of changing or developing a habit.

Routine is an action you take because of the cue. It can be a positive action you want to start doing or a negative action you must stop. If your cue is boredom, then your action may be to watch television for a short time.

Reward is the result you get from taking action. This can be positive or negative, but a healthy habit must always produce positive results. For many people, their efforts usually result in temporary happiness or a sense of fulfillment.

Six Steps to Building Healthy Habits

Building healthy habits shouldn't be a difficult task. You can simplify it further by following these steps:

1. Know the habits you want.

There are certain things you want to stop doing and others you intend to start or keep doing. When you decide to develop healthy habits, you need to know those habits you want to develop or continue. This is a fundamental step that is crucial to the success of the process.

2. Develop a plan.

Your plan consists of the various actions you will need to take to develop a habit. The actions in the plan should be realistic and sustainable to improve your chances of success. The better the plan, the easier it is to remain consistent. To develop a new behavior or habit, you can try the small changes approach. These small changes are things you can do without a significant impact on your schedule or daily routine.

3. Remain consistent.

In developing a new habit, consistency is a crucial part of its success. Being consistent involves repeating the action. Through repetition, your body will begin to act automatically once there is a cue or trigger. To ensure you remain consistent, you must include the habit-forming actions in your schedule. Actions you can add to your morning routine are often the best. These actions can be a morning jog or meditation that you perform the moment you wake up.

4. Navigate through setbacks.

Developing a new habit is a goal that you intend to achieve. When walking toward a goal, you will usually come across hindrances and setbacks. Learning to deal with these setbacks is crucial to the success of your habit formation. What you must understand is that it is okay to have a bad day—a day on which you don't perform the habit-forming action or one in which you give in to your cravings. Having a few of these days won't have a detrimental impact on the habit-forming process. There will only be an issue if these days overextend. When you fail to repeat the habit-forming process for too many days, you lose the progress you've made toward making the action automatic.

5. Give room for downtime.

Habits are important in your life, but rest is also crucial. In life, you cannot succeed if you focus solely on work without dedicating time to rest, relax, and have fun. The same applies when forming a new habit. As you try to develop new habits, make sure you create a period for downtime in your schedule. This should be a period every week during which you can relax and reflect. Reflect on how far you have come and what steps you have taken to get to this new point. Resting during this period is essential to help your body recover from the previous week's actions while regaining energy for the next week. Expressing gratitude and positivity will also help you during your rest periods.

6. Enjoy the rewards.

As you learned earlier, the rewards are the results of the action you perform. When building a new habit, there must be a reward that you intend to enjoy at the end of the process. The habit-forming process isn't complete until you get this reward, so you must take time to enjoy it.

Simplifying the Habit-Forming Process

1. Make it simple initially.

Your habits are goals that you intend to achieve. When setting goals, many individuals often make them large and complex. This is what you must avoid when setting

STEP 1—COMMIT TO TAKING ACTION | 113

your goals. In developing your habit, you must set goals that are simple and easy to achieve. You can liken this to taking baby steps. The smaller and simpler the goal or action, the more difficult it is to fail. The benefit of taking this approach is that it helps you get the action done on days when you have zero motivation. Smaller actions require less commitment in comparison to larger goals that need lots of motivation and commitment. By setting smaller goals, you improve your consistency. You should also focus on small wins, as these offer the motivation you need to take the next step.

2. Get people and allies to help.

When trying to achieve a goal or develop a new habit, having people to support you can make a huge difference. The people you choose to tell about your new habit should be those you trust. They can be your friends or family members. The idea behind telling these people about your goal is to make you accountable. When you know people are watching and taking note of your actions, it is easier to remain committed to your goals.

You can create a social media page for this purpose. Here, you will post updates on your progress for your friends and family to take note. If you feel your friends and family members won't give you the push you need, you can look for an online community with people working on the same habit or something similar. Your need to gain social approval from this online community may be what you need to develop this new habit.

3. Focus on one habit.

When planning to change your habits, you may come up with several new habits that you need to develop. Most individuals usually try to develop these habits at the same time and fail at this task. There is a simple reason for this—ego depletion. Ego depletion implies that there is a limited pool of mental resources that you can draw from using your willpower.

To complete a task, willpower is an essential factor. Focusing on multiple habits at once will drain your mental resources faster and make it challenging to complete each. When you decide to focus on a single habit, you create a reserve of willpower that you can pull from to achieve your goal. Deciding on the habit you need to focus on is essential. You will need to prioritize and focus on it until you reach the point where it becomes automatic.

4. Develop discipline.

Discipline is an essential quality you need to achieve any goal in life. In building healthy habits, discipline will pave the way for your success. Through discipline, you can learn to focus on the habit that you intend to develop. You can also develop a better work ethic when you have discipline. This improved work ethic will give you that zeal to work hard, believe in yourself, and meet every objective you set in life.

"You were never created to live depressed, defeated, guilty, condemned, ashamed or unworthy. You were created to be victorious."

— JOEL OSTEEN

STEP 2—CHANGE THE NARRATIVE

Changing the narrative is often an excellent way to deal with negativity. The narrative refers to how you engage in negative self-talk. Do you personalize situations, overgeneralize, or magnify them? To change the narrative, there are specific steps you can take.

IDENTIFY YOUR NEGATIVE THOUGHTS

The first step in changing your narrative is to identify your negative thoughts. This is something we discussed in an earlier chapter of this book. Your negative thoughts usually come in the form of misleading and unhelpful self-talk.

These are cognitive distortions that you must change, if you remember we called them the demons of our mind. Cognitive distortions imply that these thoughts are inaccurate in how they explain a situation and also unrealistic. Different forms of cognitive distortions are common, such as the following:

1. Overgeneralization: This is the process of predicting a future event using the past as the basis. In such situations, you will continue telling yourself that the same negative event will keep repeating itself because it has happened before. For example, when you miss out on a promotion at work, you may assume that you will never get a promotion if you remain in the same office.

2. Minimization: This is a form of cognitive distortion in which you always assess yourself as being inferior to others. You never place high regard on your positive qualities or strengths. This is noticeable in a situation where someone thanks you for doing something, but you say to yourself, "That is something anyone could have done."

3. Black-and-white thinking: This is a form of thinking that involves focusing on only the extremes. Here, a situation can only be good or bad; there is nothing in-between. This form of thinking is terrible because the standards you set for yourself becomes too high, and you find yourself always in a state of disappointment. For example, in an exam with grades from A to E, anything except an A is the same as an E to you.

4. *Should statements:* This is another form of cognitive distortion in which you navigate through life using "should" and "should not" statements. Why is this a problem? The problem with these statements is that they don't allow the inherent risk and uncertainty that we must experience in life. These statements give you a false sense of security that can often lead to extreme anxiety, resentment, and frustration in life. Without preparing for the possibility of failing, it is difficult to process anything that happens outside of your predictions.

5. *Personalization:* Everything that happens in life is never your sole responsibility, but this is what you assume through personalization. When you try to take responsibility for everything that occurs, you push yourself to a point where you always want to be in control. When you try to exert control over things beyond your reach, you end up experiencing anxiety and stress.

6. *Magnification:* This is the opposite of minimization. In magnification, you take note of your flaws and errors and then overstate them. As a result, minor

mistakes you make can become the focal point of your negative self-talk.

7. *Mind-reading:* This is when you assume you understand how others are thinking. There is no evidence on which you base these assumptions, which makes them inaccurate and biased. In most cases of mind-reading, your focus is usually on the negative aspects of a situation.

CHECK FOR COGNITIVE DISTORTIONS FROM OTHERS

In dealing with your cognitive distortions, you can also try identifying these distortions in other people's speech. Although you are looking to solve your problem, it is easier to identify these distortions in others than in yourself. This is because you eliminate the subjective perspective and switch to an objective view.

Looking for cognitive distortions from an objective perspective is more accurate since you solely focus on the facts presented to you. By identifying these cognitive distortions, you become more knowledgeable about what to look out for. This is the information you use in determining the cognitive distortions in your self-talk.

HAVE A CONVERSATION WITH YOUR INNER CRITIC LIKE A FRIEND

A conversation is an excellent way to deal with most problems. This is an approach you must take when dealing with your inner critic. Make the conversation seem like one with a friend.

The first thing you want to do when talking to a friend is to develop the right tone. This is the most critical step. Through the tone, you can determine if you or your inner critic is being unfair, judgmental, sarcastic, or harsh. Identifying these changes in tone requires a better understanding of yourself as an individual. You should also have a name for your inner critic. This is an essential step that helps with detachment.

The goal of this process is to resolve the issues you have with your inner critic, so one thing you must do is to listen. You must listen a lot during the initial stages of the conversation before you start engaging.

LEARN THE POWER OF CHOICE

Choosing what to do is your sole responsibility. Don't let anyone or anything take this away from you. When you take charge of your choices, it may seem like you're stepping out of your comfort zone. This is okay since it allows you to end the cycle of negativity. In ending this cycle, you must make it relative to your inner critic. To do this, you must ask questions. These questions are necessary to identify the flaws in the statements from your inner critic. The right questions will expose these statements as lies you shouldn't listen to.

SHUTTING THE INNER CRITIC BY THINKING LIKE A STOIC, ESSENTIALIST, OR MINIMALIST

The teachings of stoicism promote the idea of maintaining a rational and calm mind in every situation. Stoics are adept at paying attention to the things that are within their control and eliminating thoughts or worries regarding those beyond their control.

Negative self-talk often results when we focus on things we cannot control. One of the few things we can control is our thoughts. This means you have control over the negative self-talk in your life. If you're continually telling yourself you will fail a course, then there are certain things that you can do to avoid this outcome.

The first is to study or prepare adequately for the exam.

Another thing is to make sure you turn in all your assignments. Once you make adequate preparation and write the exam to your best capabilities, then all other things are beyond your control.

Through stoicism, you learn that while the outcomes are beyond your control, your actions and behaviors are things you can control. Therefore, you must realize that you have done your best in a situation and accept anything that happens calmly.

Another helpful thinking pattern is that of an essentialist. This is a pattern that helps you understand that you don't need to do it all. The need to do it all is one area your inner critic gets the most of you.

As an essentialist, you learn to prioritize specific tasks while you leave the others. For example, instead of focusing on completing an entire project in one go, you can break it down to smaller parts that you can focus on separately.

With the essentialist mindset, your focus shifts from getting everything done to doing the right things. The inner critic is usually emphasizing your inability to do it all. This criticism often makes it challenging to accept trade-offs.

Understanding that trade-offs serve as an essential part

of achieving the right goals makes it impossible for your inner critic to drag you back. You must understand that there is a need to choose what you can do well.

You're giving yourself the power to decide where you will focus all your energy. This will help you get the right results, reduce the impact of your inner critic, and motivate you to work harder.

The final thought pattern you can adopt is that of the minimalist. The minimalist approach to life is that of having less. They learn to live with just the things that matter most to them.

In the minimalist approach, there is a process known as decluttering. This process can be applied to your physical environment and your mind. Your inner critic is often a result of clutter in your mind.

Random thoughts that flow into your mind and speak negatively may often be a result of the things happening around you. A home that is packed with clutter will lead to a cluttered mind. The clutter makes it difficult for you to focus on the thoughts that matter most.

As a minimalist, your focus is usually on the things that give you happiness and joy. This is how they spend their time intentionally and wisely. Focusing on the things you're passionate about makes it more difficult for your inner critic to promote any form of negativity.

Minimalists also achieve a state of mind in which they learn to overcome the background noises in life. To you, this shouldn't mean blocking out your inner critic. It means pushing past the negative thoughts from the inner critic.

As you learn to push past the noise from your inner critic, its hold over you weakens to a point where it shuts down.

BREAK THE NEGATIVE SELF-TALK HABIT

Although your inner critic takes a part of the blame for the negative self-talk in your life, you also share a part of this blame. To overcome negative self-talk, you must learn to break the habit of negative self-talk.

Breaking a habit can take a while, so you must go through the process gradually. First, start by changing the language you use. Statements like "I hate" should become "I don't like." By reducing the intensity of the statements, it becomes easier to overcome the negativity.

Another action you can take is to change your perspective on certain events. If your current perspective involves looking at the impact of an issue in five years, try shifting it to two years. You may realize that you're worried about something in the distant future that may never occur.

> "*Clear thinking requires courage rather than intelligence.*"
>
> — THOMAS SZASZ

STEP 3—WRITE A THOUGHT RECORD

A thought record is a way to put down your thoughts in writing so that you have more time to assess them. The assessment of your thoughts is a crucial part of understanding them, identifying the negativity in them, relativizing, and changing these thoughts.

THE THOUGHT DIARY

A thought diary is an essential tool that you need to create thought records. Regardless of what process you choose to change your negative thinking, a thought diary will be useful. The thought records you create in your thought diary are crucial in helping you gain clarity regarding your thinking pattern and grasp your negative thoughts better.

A thought diary can also act as the final piece of the puzzle for many individuals. This is because it gives better insight into how your emotional reactions result from your thoughts and not your situation. A good thing about thought records is that you can use them to monitor changes in your self-talk.

Every week, you will surely experience more than a single situation that promotes negative self-talk. Each time you experience these situations, be sure to record what your inner critic says. To improve the accuracy of your records, you can follow the steps given in this chapter.

CREATING A THOUGHT RECORD IN SIX STEPS

Step 1: Pause

The moment you notice a change in your emotions, the first thing to do is to pause. When you pause, the first question you need to ask yourself is "What happened here?"

By answering this question, you're getting as much information as you need regarding the situation that triggered a change in your emotions. Some of the information you need to write down in your thought diary includes the following:

- The time and date of the event
- Your location during the event
- Anyone who was with you at the time of occurrence
- A summary of anything happening before the change in your emotions

Once you write these down, you have taken the first step toward creating your thought record. The information in this section will be useful to both you and your therapist later.

Step 2: Trigger

The trigger refers to what exactly led to a change in your emotions. The problem with the triggers is that it can be anything. Some of the one-word questions you need to ask include:

- Who?
- When?
- Why?
- What?
- Where?

Sometimes you may find out that you already have your trigger in your information regarding step 1. Nonetheless, it is a good idea to clarify. The trigger is often a combination of different factors, so you must answer every question on the list.

Step 3: Thoughts

Once you notice the trigger and the change in your emotions, you need to pay attention to the thoughts that run through your mind. It would help if you recorded these thoughts as soon as possible so that you don't forget. There are some questions you can ask yourself, such as:

- "What was I saying at that moment?"
- "Was there any prior thought in my mind?"
- "Did the situation have any impact on my life or future?"
- "Was I visualizing, or did I have a recollection of any picture, image, or memory before the negative thoughts?"

Step 4: Emotions

The changes in your emotions are essential in dealing with these thoughts. The emotions and sensations in your body are usually the things you assess in determining if you need to complete a thought record or not.

When determining the emotions, you should use a one-word description. Were you sad, angry, or excited? These are the simplest ways to describe your emotions in a thought record.

Next, you can record the body sensations. Some individuals might experience a contraction of the muscles, while others may choose to describe it as feeling butterflies in their stomachs. What is the sensation you feel?

The last thing you need to record is the strength of the emotion. You can rate this on a scale of 0–100. This is the intensity of the emotion you felt. There should be separate ratings in case you had several emotions.

Step 5: Alternative Thoughts

The reason for creating a thought record is that you understand that there might be a cognitive distortion in your thoughts. Therefore, it is necessary to come up with alternative thoughts that can replace them. These thoughts should be realistic in their interpretation of the situation.

Step 6: Re-Rate Your Emotions

Now that you have created the thought record, there should be changes in your emotion. The difference in your emotions should be significant since you have created alternative thoughts to your negative thoughts. This doesn't imply that you have eliminated the emotions.

It simply means that the intensity of the emotions has reduced. This is what you need to record. Re-assess the emotions, and write down what you feel is the current intensity. This assessment will help you determine the effectiveness of the alternative thoughts you provided.

"Anger, resentment and jealousy doesn't change the heart of others-- it only changes yours."

— SHANNON ALDER

STEP 4—BUILD YOUR SELF-WORTH

In learning to overcome negativity, one area that many people overlook is how they see themselves. Do you love or appreciate who you are? This is a question you must answer in your path toward overcoming negative self-talk and behaviors.

WHAT IS SELF-WORTH?

Self-worth refers to the value you place on yourself as an individual. It is your certainty that you are loved by others and have the right to be loved by them. In determining self-worth, most individuals assess themselves based on certain factors, including the following:

- Performance

- Appearance
- Achievements
- Career
- Net worth

If you take an honest review of past comparisons between yourself and another person, you will notice that one or more of these factors were used as the basis for the comparison.

When trying to get rid of negative self-talk, there are three things you must develop. These are closely related factors that play an essential role in overcoming negativity. In addition to self-worth, others include self-confidence and self-esteem.

Self-confidence is a term that describes your belief or trust in your judgment, abilities, and capabilities. As a result of an increase in your self-belief, you gain more motivation to work toward things that matter most to you, such as your goals. You also become a happier individual since you earn more success through your abilities.

Self-esteem refers to how you view yourself in terms of your self-worth. Do you appreciate who you are? This is a question that affects your self-esteem. In determining your self-esteem, it is common to assess your emotions, behavior, and appearance.

For many individuals, self-esteem can determine whether they will be successful or fail at any activity, including school and work. There is a need to have a healthy self-esteem. If your self-esteem is too high, you may find yourself being narcissistic.

BUILDING YOUR SELF-WORTH

There are different actions you can take to help develop your self-worth. There are also unhealthy habits you must break to maintain a healthy self-worth. In this section, you will learn about the various things that can help build healthy self-worth.

Avoid Linking Your Self-Worth to Your Job or Partner

A common mistake many individuals make is to use one aspect of their life as a basis for their self-worth. This aspect can be a job, a partner, and so on. This is something people with low self-esteem do.

The problem with doing this is that you avoid working on ways to feel good about yourself. Instead, you let the love of another person or your job make you feel good. So what happens when your partner leaves or you lose your job?

You should only let your job and your relationship give you pride, joy, and fulfillment. One thing they must never do is define your self-worth. Learn to see yourself as more than your job or your relationship so that you can live a better life.

Utilize the Power of Positive Affirmations

The things you tell yourself have a significant impact on your self-confidence and self-esteem. This is why you must learn to use positive affirmations. Despite the positive effects of these affirmations, they can be a problem for some individuals.

This is common among individuals with very low self-esteem. With a positive affirmation, you're saying things to push yourself toward success. The only problem with these affirmations is that they are difficult to believe, especially with low self-esteem.

Because of low self-esteem or self-confidence, it is common to misinterpret these positive affirmations. You see them as lies you tell yourself to look good. On the contrary, positive affirmations can help if you take the right approach.

The first approach is to keep repeating these positive affirmations until they become your reality. This will be possible if you can improve your self-esteem or self-worth to a point where these affirmations become realistic.

Another excellent approach is to make a few changes to positive affirmations. Adjust your affirmations to become statements that you can believe at your current level.

Stop Comparing Yourself to Others

To improve your self-worth, self-esteem, and self-confidence, you must stop the comparisons. When you compare yourself to others, there is never a positive outcome. The reason is simple.

For most individuals, the behaviors and aspects they portray in public are usually the best they have to offer. In your comparisons, you will be pitting these excellent qualities of others against your undesirable attributes. This is a recipe for disaster.

There are several disadvantages of comparisons that you need to note. One of these is that it has no end. When you start comparing yourself to others, even success won't be enough to eliminate the habit.

Another problem with comparisons is that it promotes resentment. This includes resentment toward yourself because you assume you're not good enough. Also, you begin to resent others because you feel they are better than you or have a more comfortable life.

If you have a habit of comparing yourself to others, it is

time to break this habit. To do this, there are specific actions you can take. One of these is to stop seeing life as a competition.

Understand that everyone is working separately and there is no price for moving faster than another person. You must also learn to appreciate the things you have through the practice of gratitude. When you practice gratitude, your eyes become open to the good things in your life.

Develop Thoughts That Exhibit Self-Compassion

Everyone has a few flaws they exhibit from time to time, and there are times when you make mistakes in life. How you treat yourself in these situations matter a lot. For many individuals, they usually engage in self-criticism in these situations.

Self-criticism can be a significant issue in your life since it can further damage your self-esteem. What you need to adopt is the ability to show self-compassion. When you exhibit self-compassion, you become loving, forgiving, and accepting toward yourself.

In learning to show self-compassion, several actions can help ease the process. One of these is to treat yourself in the same manner that you will treat a friend. This is because everyone always offers support and compassion when dealing with friends.

For example, when a friend is feeling down, you will usually go as far as holding their hands, using endearing words like "darling," and so on. These are actions you should direct to yourself. It is a way of showing self-kindness.

Another critical step is to learn to accept mistakes. Self-criticism makes life more difficult for you when you make mistakes. You must understand that mistakes are what make you human.

No one makes it to the top without making mistakes. These are learning opportunities that you must value in life.

Know Your Strengths and Develop Them

Despite having flaws in certain areas, you will surely be competent in so many others. Now, what you must do is to keep improving yourself in these areas. Take steps to ensure you're showcasing these strengths and developing them.

When trying to discover your strengths or competencies, you can start by taking tests. The enneagram test, Gallup StrengthsFinder 2.0, or Briggs-Meyers test can help in this situation. If these are not suitable options, then you can go to a career coach for help.

Some individuals might have strength in strategizing.

This makes it possible for them to come up with effective plans that can help achieve a goal or complete projects. For others, they can show a high level of sensory awareness.

These individuals will usually have a high level of natural confidence, avoid overanalyzing situations, and connect deeply with physical stimulus. Some people also have strengths in brainstorming, thinking, and so on.

In developing your competencies, you must make sure you build your life around them. When you perform most of your daily activities without relying on your strengths and competencies, there is an adverse effect. You will notice yourself becoming unhappy, feeling drained, and frustrated at the end of the day.

One simple step you must take is to assess your life. Identify the various activities you perform that don't fully utilize your strengths and competencies. If they are activities you can minimize, then do so, and shift your focus to those activities that require your competencies.

Learn to be Adaptable and Flexible

Adaptability is an ability that enables you to make changes that will help you fit into a new environment or overcome a current situation. The need for adaptability and flexibility is identifiable in your career, relationships, and other areas of life.

One of the benefits of being adaptable is that seeing opportunities in failures becomes a part of you. When you learn to adapt in such situations, you learn to grow as an individual. It grants you the ability to change your belief or stance regarding specific events.

This is essential in helping you accept something as being wrong despite your previous belief that it was right. Another important reason why you need to become adaptable is to know the things you can't change. By understanding that you cannot change a decision or outcome, you can adjust to your current situation and move on.

Another reason why adaptability helps is that it gives you an open mind. Most people who engage in negative self-talk have limitations in their thinking. With an open mind, you have the willingness to listen and learn from others.

Listening to others gives you a broader context, and this is essential in giving you more options. The more options you create, the more opportunities for success. When your success outweighs your failures, it becomes more challenging to engage in negative self-talk.

Let Go of Regrets and Guilt

In life, guilt and regret often serve as means through which we remain true to our values. When you find out that people are starving around the world, you may feel guilty about wasting food. This can lead to better habits, like only taking what you can eat.

Feeling guilt for acting selfishly is a good thing. Nonetheless, there is a problem with guilt, which becomes noticeable when you feel it in excess. In promoting negativity, being a perfectionist is one of the biggest challenges.

Perfectionism can lead to both guilt and self-criticism. As a perfectionist, failure to meet the standards you set for yourself makes self-criticism a norm. This is also due to a lack of flexibility and adaptability in your mindset.

Guilt and regret both go hand-in-hand because they both induce negative emotions in an individual. It is often a result of both the things you can control and those beyond your control. If something negative happens because you failed to take action or you procrastinated, then it is common to experience regret.

Harmful guilt, on the other hand, is a result of various things, such as the following:

- Seeing yourself as being better off than family

members or friends
- Being jealous of someone close to you
- Feeling like you haven't done enough for someone despite doing a lot

In identifying harmful guilt, there is one thing you must notice. This is the fact that the guilt you experience is often a result of your thoughts. Knowing this is crucial because while your thoughts can hurt you, only your actions can hurt another individual.

Therefore, you must determine if you've taken any form of action that may hurt others. If not, then there is no reason for guilt. You must also learn how to maximize the regret you experience.

Regrets often result from you focusing on the past and replaying past events in your mind. The first step to overcome these regrets is to focus on the present through mindfulness practices. Also, you can use regret as a motivation to take a new path and to correct your actions. For example, if you regret neglecting your loved one or raising your voice at them because of alcohol addiction, then use this regret as a motivation to stop your addiction.

Accept Compliments

One of the hardest things to do when you struggle with

low self-esteem is to accept compliments. The reason is that these compliments are the complete opposite of how you feel. Since you need these compliments now more than ever, you must learn how to accept them.

The first step to accepting compliments is to view them as a sincere comment from whoever is giving it. A problem many individuals with low self-esteem face is the assumption that compliments are malicious and ignorant. When you believe you're not smart, a compliment on how smart you are can quickly appear to be insincere.

You can overcome this by assessing the person giving the compliment. Is there any reason why they will intentionally try to taunt or trick you? In most cases, there is usually no reason for any of this to be the case.

Another action you can take is to try changing your thoughts when you receive a compliment. This will require a confrontation between you and your inner critic. If someone tells you that you did something good, maybe a presentation or a project, your inner critic may try to tell you it was a terrible project or presentation.

In addressing this critic, tell yourself that there are aspects you got right, which is why you're getting the compliment. Recognizing your strengths is a crucial part of this process. Most of the things you hear from your inner critic are often reflex responses to downplay any positive event.

You can also address these by coming up with positive responses. These are responses you use to accept compliments. You can use responses like "Thank you. I appreciate your kind feedback."

These responses make it difficult to deny the compliments you receive.

Don't Try to Be Like Everyone Else

Trying to be like everyone else is often a step many people take to gain approval. A problem with this approach is that it negatively affects your self-esteem and self-confidence. When you start adopting the traits of others, you slowly lose sight of who you are, and you find it difficult to love yourself.

To build your self-worth, you must first learn to love yourself. This means accepting all your flaws and negative behaviors. Stop the habit of trying to please others at the expense of your standards, values, and happiness.

As you journey through life, you will meet lots of people. Some will like you, while others won't, and that's okay. When you try too hard to be loved by all, it becomes harder for people to like you.

"*Much unhappiness has come into the world because of bewilderment and things left unsaid.*"

— FYODOR DOSTOEVSKY

STEP 5—COMMUNICATE

"If you want to go fast, go alone. If you want to go far, go together." This is a quote you may have come across in your lifetime. So what does it mean to you?

Many people will interpret it differently, and a straightforward interpretation is that working with others is a prerequisite for attaining the peak. When you work alone, you may feel you aren't being pulled back by others' actions, but there is so much you can do when you work with others.

Everyone has their strengths and weaknesses. This is why you need other people to help even the odds. On the topic of communication, here are some things you must always remember:

1. You are never alone.

It doesn't matter the type of struggles you're going through; there is always someone to help. This can be your friends, family, therapist, or someone in a similar situation. All you need to do is open up and let someone know.

It may be difficult at first, but having someone you can talk to will make the burden a lot lighter. When dealing with negative emotions, interacting with other people can change the way you view certain situations.

Your friends and family are usually the most helpful group in this situation. They consist of individuals you trust and allies you know can get you through the tough times.

2. Speak honestly.

When talking about your feelings and getting over negative emotions, you must communicate clearly. Speaking honestly is the only way you can achieve clarity. Let your family, friends, or allies know when you are not okay.

If you say you're okay when you're not, no one will be able to help you. In most cases, people will avoid putting pressure on you to know what's going on. Everyone will assume you're not comfortable sharing these details with them. When this happens, you are left alone to deal with your problems, even if you can't.

3. *Try speaking out loud.*

An excellent strategy in dealing with negative thoughts is to say them out loud. When you continuously repeat these thoughts out loud, they slowly lose their effect on you. One way this happens is that you start to notice the absurdity in these thoughts.

4. *Stop repressing your emotions.*

When dealing with negative thoughts and emotions, many people opt to repress these emotions and thoughts. Although it may seem like a good idea, repressing them has more negative effects. There was an article in *The Atlantic* regarding this issue.

According to the article, several studies connect long life to emotional expression and repressed emotions to increased stress. This implies that repressing your feelings causes more stress in your life and reduces your life span.

Actions such as drug use, excess alcohol consumption, and an increase in screen time can be signs of repressed emotions. If you're exhibiting any of these signs, you must learn how to deal with your feelings correctly.

LEARNING TO MANAGE NEGATIVE EMOTIONS

There are various types of emotions we experience as humans. You can experience love, relief, contentment, worry, pride, anxiety, relief, and fear. Regardless of the feelings you experience, positive or negative, you must understand the right way to deal with them.

Maintaining a balance is crucial when dealing with your emotions. There is no room for extremes in this case. However, achieving this balance can be difficult.

In the world today, various issues can push you to the negative extreme of your emotions. Examples are the loss of a family member or a job. Without a proper handle on your emotions, these issues can have other negative impacts like insomnia, depression, heart problems, and anxiety.

In learning to handle these emotions appropriately, there are certain things you can do. These include the following:

Seek Professional Help

When you have problems dealing with your emotions, talking to a professional is always an excellent option. These individuals have the skills and experience to help you overcome your current predicament.

Go for Therapy

In dealing with negative emotions, one option that remains relevant is therapy. There is a higher chance of overcoming your issues through therapy in comparison to the use of medication. Therapy provides an opportunity for you to learn a lot more about who you are as an individual, improve all areas of your life, and minimize distress.

There are different types of therapy you can engage in when dealing with your negative emotions. Your therapist will usually decide on the right option, but here are some things you should know about these various types.

1. Cognitive behavioral therapy (CBT). When you decide to go for CBT, you allow yourself to learn about how your behavior, thoughts, and feelings relate. It is a therapy that aims to create a balance in the way you think by helping you visualize your life, situations, and yourself from multiple perspectives. The goal of these steps is to give you the motivation to challenge your thinking. When you learn to challenge your thinking, you can learn to rephrase every negative self-talk and thoughts that drag you down. A good thing about this form of therapy is that you also get to work on yourself even at home. The CBT program is an excellent option for dealing with depression, anxiety, and also in anger management. To complete the program, six sessions are usually enough.

2. Integrative therapy: If you want a flexible form of therapy, then integrative therapy is a great option. The counselor in an integrative therapy session understands that each individual is unique. These unique qualities of individuals create differences in how each person should approach their challenges. Based on your needs as the client, the integrative counselor will come up with a combination of techniques, carefully selected from the different forms of therapy available.

3. Person-centered therapy: This is a method that focuses on helping you understand yourself and your feelings on a deeper level. One of the benefits of an excellent person-centered therapy session is that you will never feel like you're being criticized. This form of therapy will leave you in a state where you're fit to retain a balance of your emotions.

4. Gestalt therapy: In this form of therapy, you will gain a deeper understanding of the relationship between your intense feelings and body movement. Your therapist will push you to a point where you begin to open up and accept the feelings you have buried deep inside. Gestalt therapy is one with a focus on developing your self-awareness.

5. Psychodynamic therapy: Psychodynamic therapy is one of the most useful treatment methods for dealing with your negative thoughts, behaviors, and emotions. This form of treatment focuses on navigating to the root of the problems. These roots often dwell in our past.

The feelings you will discover through psychodynamic therapy include those you are conscious of and those you are not. It requires a long commitment since the treatment can go on for years. This is a significant discomfort with psychodynamic therapy.

Find a Support Group

Another beneficial method of dealing with negative behaviors is by joining a support group. A support group consists of individuals who are currently facing a specific problem and those who have overcome the same problem.

These groups are useful because individuals understand what each person is going through. This understanding makes it easier for every member of the group to offer helpful advice and emotional support to whoever needs it.

There are different types of support group, and each one may have a unique structure. Some support groups offer face-to-face meetings, while others may focus on an online community. You can also find a few that offer both options.

These groups are often run by hospitals, clinics, community organizations, or nonprofits. Depending on how the group is set up, you may get to listen to experienced professionals like psychologists, social workers, nurses, and doctors.

When you decide to join a support group, there are several benefits and several drawbacks you should know about. Some of the benefits include the following:

- You have the opportunity to stay motivated while handling your challenges.
- You have a platform to express your feelings honestly and openly.
- You learn new skills that will help in dealing with challenges.
- You minimize the depression, fatigue, and stress you experience.
- You eliminate the feeling of isolation and loneliness you feel.

The following are some of the drawbacks of joining a support group:

- Your information is usually not confidential.
- Some individuals will make it a competition to determine who has the worst experience or condition.
- Interpersonal conflict and group tension are common.
- Some members can be disruptive.
- There is a possibility of hearing medical advice that is inappropriate or untested.

In addition to this, you should also take care when joining an online community. Since most of these communities interact mainly through texts, it is common to have misunderstandings in the group. If you decide to join a support group, you can ask your doctor, hospital, or clinic for information.

"Feelings come and go like clouds in a windy sky. Conscious breathing is my anchor."

— THICH NHAT HANH

STEP 6—PRACTICE MINDFULNESS AND MEDITATION

Most people only understand how meditation can motivate a peaceful lifestyle and promote physical well-being. I think this proves how little the number of people is who truly know the full benefit of meditation and mindfulness-based activities. Those who practice mindfulness and meditation have long since claimed its mental and psychological effects.

Meditation is an age-long practice. However, that does not bring us any closer to understanding all of its effects and benefits on the mind. Only as recently as 2011, a study carried out at the Massachusetts General Hospital by a Harvard-affiliated research team led by Sara Lazar proved that mindfulness meditation resulted in changes in brain structure.

The structural differences in the brain's gray matter produced over time by meditation lead to improvements in a lot of cognitive and psychological functions of a practitioner. The lesson you should learn here is that understanding what meditation is, how to practice it, when and where to do it, what it can do for you can improve your self-esteem and enable a more positive thinking habit. We've got the science to prove it.

In this chapter, we discuss the sixth step to overcoming your negative self-talk. Practicing mindfulness and meditation has the potential to turn your habit of self-loathing, wallowing, low self-esteem, and self-doubt into a mentality of positivity. Cultivating this positivity and making sure to avoid your triggers will create a lasting process of alignment.

Let's begin by learning what meditation means. Then we'll focus on mindfulness and how your well-being can benefit from practicing it.

MEDITATION

Meditation is, ultimately, a self-awareness exercise. It is an experience that results in self-consciousness and self-improvement skills with long practice. When you practice meditation, your aim is to think deeply and train the mind to focus on self-discovery. By discovering it, you will learn to experience the present moment with great calm. Moreover, your mental and physical well-being will be in great condition.

It is quite difficult to control everything that happens to you. To even try will result in depression, anxiety, low self-confidence, and self-loathing. What you have the power to do, however, is to control how you respond to the sensations and feelings you experience. Recognizing these feelings and what they mean to you gives you greater power to control your response to them.

Meditation is about gaining clarity. It is not just about clearing the mind to empty it. It involves clearing the mind to enable it to concentrate on the objective. Through meditation, you can gain an understanding of yourself, thoughts, personality, behavior, and environment. This understanding can then lead to positivity, self-love, relaxation and stress-relief, emotional well-being, and concentration.

Types of Meditation

Because of the differences in lifestyles, emotional intelligence, and cognition, different types of meditation produce different results in most people. There are, however, numerous techniques of meditation that you can tailor to your needs. In a broad classification, depending on the desired outcome of a routine, meditation can either be as follows:

- Focused-attention meditation
- Open-monitoring meditation

Focused-attention meditation involves the meditation routines that concentrate your attention on a singular trigger. It could be an object, breathing, a sound or mantra, or even a mental visualization. The purpose of this is to get the mind to concentrate on this singular motivation while blocking out every other sensation around and within it. This style of meditation helps the mind overcome worry and distractions and improves focus, memory, and calmness.

Open-monitoring meditation is a style of meditation that enables a wide consciousness of every aspect of yourself and your environment, including your response to it. It focuses not only on your thought but also on your thought habit (the way you think). The benefits of this style include improved self-awareness, self-reflection, self-control, emotional intelligence, and stress-relief.

When we take a closer look at both styles of meditation, we can identify several techniques of meditation arising from them. Each technique is based on either focused-attention meditation or open-monitoring meditation. They all help to develop a definite aspect of yourself.

Meditation can also be calming or insightful. Calming meditation helps you to foster a sense of calm and peace in your mind and body. This results in improved concentration and stress-handling abilities. Calming meditations are usually focused-attention meditations.

Insightful meditation focuses on reflecting on and learning from your sensations and feelings you experience. This self-reflection builds self-awareness and transforms the thought process. As a result, the person becomes more compassionate and wiser.

Other forms of meditation like Zen meditation, mantra, yoga, transcendental meditation, Vipassana meditation, Qigong meditation, chakra meditation, and sound bath are either one or a combination of the insightful or calming meditations.

Guided or Unguided

When you're thinking of meditation to improve self-awareness, self-esteem, positive thinking habit, and mindfulness, you may choose guided meditation or unguided meditation.

As simple as it sounds, practicing guided meditation means that you're not going through the process alone.

You have help in the form of a meditation or spiritual guide who is more experienced than you are. This person is in charge of leading you through the meditation process—either personally or in a group exercise.

You can hire a guide for private meditation in your home. This is not financially easy. You can also go to a wellness center for group meditation or class. Using the guided meditation method has its benefits, and one of them is that you'll be led through meditation in the most productive way. This is essential for a beginner who just started practicing meditation.

Unguided meditation is the one you do on your own without aid from any guide. This method allows you to meditate within your comfort area without intrusion by someone else. It also allows you to modify your preferred technique to suit your need and to meditate at your own pace.

Whichever method of meditation you choose, get the most out of your practice by learning how to practice meditation and mindfulness-based activities.

How to Start Practicing Meditation

The specific detail of what your meditation routine should be like depends on the type of meditation technique you choose or need. However, there are general steps that are common to all techniques. If you have never practiced meditation before, you may find it a bit difficult to keep all of the steps of a particular routine in mind. This is normal.

The most wonderful thing about meditation is that it requires no tools or equipment. You only need yourself, your mind, your love for your well-being, and your dedication to building a happy, fulfilled life. This is what makes meditation a simple yet potent remedy for negativity and cognitive inertia.

However, if you're just starting, take all the help you can get by planning out your routine with a meditation guide. You can have the steps and routines written down so you can stay focused until you have mastered your technique.

For most meditation techniques, these basic guidelines will help you achieve and maintain a mental state of inactivity.

1. Set aside a time and place.

Meditation works best if it has become a habit. Building a habit is easier when a particular thing is done repetitively in a regular manner. Try to meditate at a specific time of the day. If you have to work till late in the day and then come home tired, you must set a time in the morning.

Choosing a particular spot to meditate helps you achieve concentration faster, and it builds a positive vibe you can rely on in that area. It could be a corner of your bedroom or your study facing the window. It could even be your basement or outside in the backyard. Wherever you have chosen as your meditation "temple," it is important that you maintain it.

2. Adopt a comfortable position.

Except when you're doing yoga or other forms of meditation that don't require it, you're most likely going to just remain in a particular position for as long as 15–20 minutes when you meditate. You must assume a comfortable position to avoid having to focus on pain and stress areas in your body.

If you use a chair, make sure to sit comfortably with your torso held upright and not slouched to one direction or the other. Otherwise, sit on the ground, preferably on a soft patch of lawn, or place a cushion underneath you.

3. Maintain external and internal concentration.

You can do this by focusing on your objective, shutting out external stimuli, and clearing your mind of worries and distractions. If you're using an object, focusing on it will help you maintain your concentration. You can close your eyes and focus inward. Think about centering yourself. A wandering mind is normal for any person practicing meditation; however, maintaining consciousness of yourself will help you gently center your mind.

4. Practice controlled breathing.

Assume a rhythm in your breathing. Take slow, deep, and regular breaths. This gives your mind something to focus on while it works on concentrating on the objective. Let your regular breathing be all you feel around you. Focus on breathing in the calm and freshness of the gentle breeze and breathing out the current of your thoughts and negativity.

You will no longer be just a beginner if you practice meditation in this way for a few weeks. It is also important you monitor your progress. Notice changes in your thought habits and clarity and try to write them in a journal. When you use meditation for decision-making, have a journal or a note with you to write down what you've decided on while you meditate.

Building a Habit of Meditation

Meditation can only be effective and produce the right results if you do it the right way. It can be quite challenging getting used to your meditation routine and schedule. Even people who are experts manage by great focus and sheer force of will. However, if you make meditation a habit, it will open up the door to an easy and more peaceful life.

As a beginner, the common hindrances you'll face when meditating will be easily avoided if you follow this guideline on how to meditate the right way. This is generally aimed at helping you build a habit of meditating. How often you meditate determines how extensive the psychological change produced by mindfulness-based meditation will be.

You should know that a person can relapse into a dangerous habit if they haven't cultivated a healthy one to replace it. A daily habit of meditation will keep you aware and mindful of every present moment. Try to meditate in the same place and at the same time. Create a serene environment where you're comfortable, safe, and at peace. It is preferable to meditate in the morning when it's calm and you're refreshed by sleep. However, if this is not possible, pick a time of the day and keep to it.

It is also important to monitor how long you spend meditating and ensure this does not decrease. You may begin by meditating for 15–20 minutes, and when you have become comfortable with that, then you may increase the time. This will help you form a meditation habit quicker.

Avoid distractions and interruptions. When you have to begin your meditation routine again after interruptions, you spend a lot of time doing it. Distractions make you lose concentration and give your mind the chance to wander. You will eventually get to the stage where you'll be able to meditate anywhere no matter how many distractions are around, but until that time, find the quietest place to meditate.

Keep away from televisions and other gadgets that might draw your attention. Unless your routine involves soothing sounds and recorded chants, avoid meditating in the vicinity of sound players. Ensure to have your phone at a safe distance.

The posture you adopt when practicing mindfulness-based meditation is important. The best thing to do is to maintain a particular comfortable posture whenever you meditate. Changing postures limits your brain's recognition and tampers with the habit-forming process.

Mindfulness is what you're aiming at. Assess yourself emotionally and physically to take stock of what has changed and what needs to still be worked on. To be sure you have achieved your goal, have a clear line of action on how to implement what you have developed during meditation. Try as much as possible to be conscious and mindful throughout the day.

MINDFULNESS

Mindfulness is self-consciousness. It is the ability to engage in an activity or thought with full awareness of what you're doing, for what reason you're doing it, and what you aim to achieve. Being mindful is being present in mind and body. It excludes loss of attention, wandering, general hyperactivity, and forgetfulness.

Improving mindfulness is possible, and you can work toward it. A person who tends to wander in thoughts and actions can overcome these attributes and increase mindfulness and focus. You can become free from distractions and become more aware of your feelings and actions without being so fixated on them. Trading mindfulness for over-compulsion is not progress.

A less-mindful person will find it difficult to achieve a lot at work, at home, or in a relationship. You find it hard to relate well with people or show sympathy and kindness if you're not mindful enough. You also get carried away in your thoughts. That way, you'll focus on and continue a strain of negative thoughts without even realizing it.

The common way to spot a less-mindful person is by interrupting them. If you find it difficult to continue a train of thought or an action when interrupted, then it probably means you were not focused in the first place.

Mindfulness differs from meditation in that it is a present state of mind that ought to be permanent. Just like your personality, mindfulness should enable you to detach from any temporary state of mind (which can be illusions, fantasy or reflection, or negative rumination) and be in the present moment. Mindfulness is a quality that we can improve through meditation.

Mindfulness-Based Activities

Meditation is your best bet for learning mindfulness. During meditation, you can train your mind whether or not to concentrate on a particular sensation. This gives you control, self-awareness, and focus. Sometimes, meditation is used to reflect and self-evaluate. In this process, you're building up mindfulness.

Research has proven that meditation can change the structure of the brain. That way, mindfulness-based activities, when practiced regularly and frequently, build up a habit that will improve not only self-consciousness but also other physical, cognitive, and psychological qualities.

These mindfulness-based activities will help you become more aware of yourself.

1. *Focused attention and noting:* This activity focuses the mind on a particular sensation, object, or

your breathing. Focused attention helps you become more aware, and noting helps you to learn more about your habits and how to control them. This could be useful for overcoming addictions.
2. *Body scan:* Uses meditation to achieve a mind-body focus that greatly improves stress-relief and affects the way we deal with pain.
3. Other mindfulness activities like visualization and reflection boost emotional intelligence and improve interpersonal relationships and compassion.

BENEFITS OF PRACTICING MINDFULNESS AND MEDITATION

Being aware and mindful of your feelings, thoughts, and moods in the present moment gives you the ability to know how to handle them. This allows you to avoid getting carried away. Selfishness and every other self-centered tendency can be overcome by practicing mindfulness.

Levels of compassion, sympathy, and consideration will be greatly improved when you focus on becoming more mindful. This will, in turn, improve your emotional intelligence. Self-awareness and focus can be improved by practicing mindfulness. Negative self-talk can also be overcome by practicing mindfulness. You have to recognize negative trains of thought, accept them, and move on toward more positive thoughts.

When you practice mindfulness and meditation the right way, the benefits will include a higher level of self-esteem. This will affect your level of self-love and confidence. Practicing meditation and mindfulness helps you to maintain focus and reduces the chances of memory loss associated with aging. It reverses mind-wandering and patterns of worry in the brain by triggering changes in the structure of the brain.

Your emotional well-being improves when you meditate regularly and the right way. Study shows signs of lower depression, anxiety, fear, and feelings of loneliness in steady practitioners of meditation than in people who do not meditate.

Mindfulness-based meditation improves your physical well-being by relieving stress and overcoming feelings of burn-out. It helps with relaxation and healthy sleep. Meditation can help you navigate the demands of a stressful job. It also helps to control blood pressure and how your body responds to pain.

HOW TO TRANSFORM NEGATIVE THOUGHT THROUGH MINDFULNESS

To transform your thoughts, you need to understand them first. Once you have understood a particular train of thought or habit as negative, then it is easy to overcome or control it. By practicing mindfulness, you may transform those negative thoughts and thought habits to neutral or positive thoughts.

In three easy steps, you can gain control of your thoughts and transform them into positives.

Step 1: Recognize the thought. Be mindful of your feelings and environment. Mindfulness helps you to be alert in order to notice when thoughts begin to take form in your mind. Most times, we follow a train of thought and begin to ruminate on it without realizing it. If the thought "I can't do it" or "This is impossible to do" comes into your mind, be mindful enough to be aware and conscious of it.

Step 2: Release the thought. One of the effects of negative thinking is cognitive inertia. This will have an outcome on your body that is unhealthy, leaving you focused and ruminating on the negative thought. Relaxing your body through a breathing exercise releases the tension and helps you think clearly. By this process also, you're able to move on to the third step.

Step 3: Change it to a positive thought. Affirming a positive version of the original thought completely cancels out the negative thought. Sometimes, you may feel reluctant to do that. That's okay. You may start by accepting a neutral version. Instead of thinking "I can't do this," you can ask "How can I do this?" This allows you to focus on how to resolve whatever difficulty you might be feeling at the moment instead of remaining in a state of paralysis.

TAKING ADVANTAGE OF TECHNOLOGY

A way to practice guided meditation as a beginner is by using meditation apps. This is cheaper and allows you to meditate in your own time within your area of comfort. You also get the help you need to get the most out of your practice.

Most apps will require you to pay a subscription fee, which is usually affordable. However, a few free apps are available for you to use, especially when starting meditation.

You can also monitor your progress. Keep a note of your decisions and actions to take by writing them in mobile journal apps, or use a voice recorder to keep voice notes while you meditate.

No matter which meditation technique works for you,

ensure that you practice meditation the right way by building focus and concentration on what you desire to change. Concentrating on your objective and tracking your progress enables you to build the desired positive mindset and thought behavior to overcome your negative self-talk.

"Take care of your body. It's the only place you have to live."

— JIM ROHN

STEP 7—TAKE CARE OF YOUR BODY

How confident are you in your body? Do you feel that your body image affects your self-esteem in any way?

Studies have proven that one's body image, essentially a perception of their physical self and feelings that result from that perception, is linked to their level of self-esteem. Body image is mostly influenced by a lot of factors ranging from comments from friends to media depictions.

When you begin to compare your body to what you see in commercials and social media and it doesn't fit, your mind will begin to create a poor body image. This causes low self-esteem and a lot of negative declarations. The question becomes, how do you get over this mindset, become comfortable with your body, and start developing your self-esteem?

BUILDING A POSITIVE MINDSET BY TAKING CARE OF YOUR BODY

First, you must understand that your body and mind are interrelated. The state of your mind affects your body (in terms of posture, physical health, and appearance). In the same way, the condition you leave your body has tremendous implications on your mental well-being.

You cannot have a healthy mindset if your body is in poor condition and vice versa. It is difficult to feel confident in yourself without an adequate amount of self-love. It is also difficult to take care of the body if you don't feel good about yourself.

Ultimately, self-esteem—how you feel about yourself and how you value yourself—has its boundaries within the mind. However, because your mind pays attention to external details, it allows your perception of your body to regulate its response. This is why body-shaming is just as dangerous as racism.

This implies that you have to get comfortable with your body and love it to build a healthy self-esteem. We have already established how important your level of self-esteem is to you overcoming your negative self-talk and building your mentality around positivity.

Countless studies have shown improvements in calmness, control, depression, and self-awareness in people undergoing active body improvement and mindfulness exercises. It is important to realize that the purpose of this step is to get comfortable with your body, see its beauty, and love it as it is. And then take active steps toward healthy living. It is not to motivate you into body modification.

The subsequent section discusses various ways through which you can keep your body in good, lovable shape and get rid of negative self-talk while at it.

HOW TO TAKE CARE OF THE BODY

Get Enough Sleep

Sleep is a natural process that allows the body and mind to relax and refresh. About seven to nine hours of sleep are recommended for the average adult to keep performance at an optimum level. The busy nature of everyday life has made sleep deprivation common as a way of getting more work done.

Lack of quality sleep, however, poses some health risks. It can affect you mentally and physically. Sleep deprivation increases the chances of cardiovascular disease. Aside from the health risks, it is also known to cause higher stress levels and sensitivity. Moreover, it can cause depression and low self-esteem in individuals.

A good night's sleep will require more than just putting in seven to nine hours of sleep. Below are several other ways you can improve the quality of sleep you are getting.

1. Try to regulate your sleep by developing a routine for it and being consistent with your sleeping and waking time daily. You may consider this as building a new habit. Habits take at least 21 days to build, and developing a new habit helps to build confidence and self-esteem.
2. Minimize the intake of food that contains caffeine as caffeine can affect sleeping patterns. Caffeine stays active in the body for at least three hours, so taking chocolates, coffee, soda, energy drinks directly before going to sleep is unhealthy. If you must indulge in taking them, do so early enough so your system is rid of their effects before sleep.
3. Exposure to lights from screens, such as TVs, phones, and computers, can also affect sleeping patterns. Avoid using these gadgets until you're

sleepy. Rather, take the time to unwind and do some mindful meditation, as this can help reduce stress.
4. Make your room sleep-enhancing. That is, cool, organized, and dark or low-light. This is easier for you to sleep.

Eat Healthily

You probably have heard that there is a relation between what you eat and how you feel about yourself. Generally, a healthy diet can reduce depression and improve your mood, while certain food can induce fatigue, raise your level of depression, and foster self-doubt.

You're learning about eating healthy in this chapter because of the obvious relationship between your food choices and your physical well-being. The type of food you eat most of the time will affect your health. However, it is also unhealthy to overstress and watch incessantly everything that you eat. Try to maintain a calm control on your diet—that's what matters most. Exercise the discipline to eat only what's good for you.

What essentially consists of a healthy diet? How can you make healthy food choices that affect your physical and mental health positively? What comes to your mind when a healthy diet is mentioned? Do you think of whole foods? Does your idea of a healthy diet include carb considerations? Diets may vary from person to person due to age, health condition, or lifestyle choices, but there are general guidelines for what a healthy diet is.

1. A healthy diet will consist basically of a variety of food from all the food groups. Such a diet provides your body with the nutrients it needs to function properly.
2. Eat enough fruits and vegetables, about three to five servings per day, as they contain lots of fiber, nutrients, and oxidants.
3. Eat meals that are low in carbohydrates and nutrient-rich.
4. Foods that contain trans-fat and refined sugars and are genetically modified are not bad for your health when eaten out in moderation.

If you need more recommendations on how to maintain a healthy diet, consult a nutritionist. A dieting routine can also be developed to match you personally.

Sweat It Out

I met a client who had anxiety problems that were often a source of depression. As a result, he had low self-esteem. During our discussions, he emphasized a lot on how uncomfortable he was with his body. So as part of the therapy I prescribed, he had to run daily.

The logic behind this is just simple science. Regular exercises and workouts affect glandular portions of the brain. Studies have proved that people who work out are not only healthier but also happier, more content, confident, calm, in control, and positive toward life than people who do not and are especially in a stressful job.

It will not be easy getting used to any exercise routine because the body has a way of avoiding exertion. However, when you have built up an exercise habit, getting a workout done daily will give you the boost in self-esteem that you desire. Building a workout habit requires discipline and dedication. So these are two other attributes you'll improve on while exercising.

When you set up a workout routine, don't think it has to be rigorous. It could be a brisk walk, jogging, weightlifting, swimming, and others. It just has to be an activity you enjoy doing as you're more likely to stick to it that way. Also, engaging in the same exercise always can turn out to require greater motivation, so you have to switch it up sometimes and try new things.

Some forms of yoga can also be considered as exercise. Aside from the benefits that come from physically exerting oneself, it is also a form of meditation that is known to help relieve stress and anxiety.

Aside from the health and mental benefits of exercise, you gain confidence from the good condition of your body and the strength you build from exercising.

Another way through which exercising builds your self-esteem is that it gives you a sense of accomplishment as it involves setting and achieving successive goals. The goal could be to lift heavier weights or run a mile longer. Achieving a set goal bolsters your confidence and makes you set your sights on achieving bigger goals.

Practice Mindfulness

Mindfulness is simply being aware of the present moment, your thoughts, and your environment. Mindfulness requires one to take an unbiased and nonjudgmental stance on the thoughts that come to mind. The practice is recommended by lots of psychologists worldwide for its benefits.

Mindfulness poses so many benefits, one being that it alleviates stress. In practicing mindfulness, your attention is shifted from the various thoughts that run through your mind, and you can focus on the present. The ability to focus on the present causes improved productivity. Also, this goes a long way to build your self-esteem.

Building mindfulness requires a great deal of patience as it doesn't happen overnight. To make the development of the habit easier, you can incorporate it into your daily routine and build it into a lifestyle. Another way to build mindfulness is by practicing gratitude. This allows you to observe and introspect deeply, finding the things you should be grateful for.

If you need to, study the previous chapter on practicing mindfulness and meditation again and more closely. Implement what you have learned. Start your mindfulness and meditation practice today.

Hydrate

The human body needs a lot more water than food. It is recommended that you drink about two liters of water each day. This will vary depending on weather conditions and physical state, say if one is exercising. Good enough, the water content of foods and beverages, such as coffee, are included in the count.

Regular consumption of water keeps one in good physical and mental state. As stated earlier, this reduces stress, puts one in good moods, and boosts self-confidence and self-esteem.

Toxins are produced in the body during metabolic processes, from dead cells through stress and even the air we breathe. Detoxifying the body regularly cleanses the body of these toxins and renews it. Water is a great detoxifying agent and should be consumed regularly. Staying hydrated regularly reduces the risk of dehydration, which can lead to confusion, headaches, and irritation. Regular consumption of water also keeps one fit for longer, and it keeps the skin hydrated and looking younger.

As a guide, if you find it difficult to drink sparkling water or table water as it is, you should consider mineral water or other forms of sweetened water. Alternatively, nutritionists advise that you could also "eat" your daily requirements in water. This will involve eating a lot of foods (fruits mostly) that have high water content—e.g., watermelons, oranges, and cucumbers. Also, avoid excessive proteins as they dehydrate the body during digestion.

Spend Time in Nature

Five studies were conducted by researchers at three European universities, and these were published in the journal *Body Image*. In three studies, some British students were presented with images of natural and built environments. Results showed that being exposed to images of natural environments and not built ones can increase body image! On the other hand, the two other studies covered participants who were made to walk in a natural or built environment. Results showed that walking in a natural environment led to a drastically higher state body appreciation while walking in a constructed environment brought about drastically lower scores. In essence, spending time in natural environments can increase body image!

The reason for this is that being around nature increases cognitive ability and neural activity, and it provides therapeutic sights—the setting sun, for example. Engaging in this activity comes in many forms, such as taking a hike, sitting by a water body, or working in a garden.

CONCLUSION

All journeys must come to an end, even the amazing ones. Like I promised, I have covered in detail all you need to correct those negative thoughts and transform them into healthier and more positive ones.

However, you need to remember that you can't change those negative thoughts without putting in the effort. You will need to invest your time and stay committed to the task. The seven-step system is not an automatic solution, but I can assure you that the outcome is worth all the effort.

Note that negative thoughts are not entirely bad. They have protected our ancestors all through evolution and helped them stay away from danger. It only becomes a problem when you do it in excess and you allow it to affect your entire life.

Remember that mistakes can occur during the process, and you may find yourself turning to those negative thoughts you are trying so hard to correct. If this happens, don't beat yourself about it because mistakes are a part of the process. The important thing is that you remember to pick yourself back up and continue on the proper track.

I would love to hear from you on what truly helped you and inspired you to become a better person. **If this has helped you in anyway please take a moment to leave a review** so I may know how it has. I may not know who you are in person, but I would be surely thrilled to know that I was able to pass on knowledge that went on to change someone's life.

Thank you for letting me guide you with my experience. I hope you get the results you want after reading this book. See you at the top of all those negative thoughts living the positive life you desire.

The Daily Morning Habit Checklist

(Don't Finish Your Morning Without This)

THIS CHECKLIST INCLUDES:

- 8 Habits you cannot take out of your morning routine.
- 8 Reasons why it will change your mood about your day.
- Implement these habits within the first hour of waking up.

The last thing we want is your day ruined because you didn't have the best start.
To receive your Daily Morning Habit Checklist, Visit this link (PS: It's Free):

https://tinyurl.com/HabitChecklist

RESOURCES

Baer, D. (2016, September 23). *The right way(s) to do introspection*. The Cut. https://www.thecut.com/2016/09/the-right-way-s-to-do-introspection.html

Counselling Directory. (2014, May 23). *Managing negative emotions*. https://www.counselling-directory.org.uk/memberarticles/managing-negative-emotions

Crespo, R. (2019, November 6). *9 minimalist values to live by*. Minimalism Made Simple. https://www.minimalismmadesimple.com/home/minimalist-values

Cuncic, A. (2019, July 13). *How to change your negative thought patterns when you have SAD*. Very Well Mind. https://www.verywellmind.com/how-to-change-negative-thinking-3024843

Eliasben. (n.d.). The psychology of habits: How to form habits (and make them stick). http://routineexcellence.com/psychology-of-habits-form-habits-make-stick/

Eurich, T. (2017, June 2). *The right way to be introspective (yes, there's a wrong way)*. TED. https://ideas.ted.com/the-right-way-to-be-introspective-yes-theres-a-wrong-way/

Exploring Your Mind. (2018, April 12). *The benefits of being committed people.* https://exploringyourmind.com/the-benefits-of-being-committed-people/

Goldstein, E. (2018, August 15). *3 mindful ways to transform negative thoughts.* Mindful. https://www.mindful.org/3-simple-ways-transform-negative-thoughts/

Grant, E. T. (2018, November 14). *7 habits you don't realize can cause your negative self-talk.* Bustle. https://www.bustle.com/p/7-habits-you-dont-realize-can-cause-your-negative-self-talk-13137479

Grohol, J. M. (2019, June 24). *15 common cognitive distortions.* Psych Central. https://psychcentral.com/lib/15-common-cognitive-distortions/

Kamb, S. (2019, December 30). *How to build healthy habits (5 hacks for habit building).* Nerd Fitness. https://www.nerdfitness.com/blog/how-to-build-healthy-habits-that-stick/

Pennycooke, M. (2017, September 4). *8 dangers of negative self-talk.* https://makedapennycooke.com/8-dangers-negative-self-talk/

Power of Positivity. (2019, June 23). *3 reasons people have negative thoughts.* https://www.powerofpositivity.com/3-reasons-negative-thoughts/

Smith, E. M. (n.d.). *What is negative thinking? How it destroys your mental health.* Healthy Place https://www.healthyplace.com/self-help/positivity/what-is-negative-thinking-how-it-destroys-your-mental-health

Smith, E. M. (n.d.). *Why am I so negative and angry and depressed?* Healthy Place. https://www.healthyplace.com/self-help/positivity/why-am-i-so-negative-and-angry-and-depressed

Wiest, B. (2019, July 18). *How to flush negative emotions from your body.* Medium. https://medium.com/@briaeliza/how-to-flush-negative-emotions-from-your-body-2b73264ad018

www.ingramcontent.com/pod-product-compliance
Lightning Source LLC
Chambersburg PA
CBHW031151020426
42333CB00013B/610